Babe ☆ Baby Doll ☆ Bambazoola ☆
Brieu ☆ Charisma ☆ Casey ☆ C
Chappie ☆ Charlie ☆ Chico ☆ Clai
Countach ☆ Cover Girl ☆ Cowboy ☆ C
Dodger ☆ Donna ☆ Double Take ☆ D
Ellie ☆ Essex ☆ Exhort (Skeeter)
Fleet ☆ Fresca ☆ Gallo ☆ Gigi ☆
Granville ☆ Hank ☆ Hanna ☆ Happy ☆ Harley ☆ Harry ☆ Heiden
Hope ☆ Hummer ☆ Immie ☆ Indy ☆ Irish ☆ Isabelle ☆ Jake
James ☆ Javelin ☆ Jenny ☆ Jim ☆ Johnny ☆ Joker ☆ Joy ☆ Junior
Keanan ☆ Kennedy ☆ Key Note ☆ Kip ☆ Kobi ☆ Lad ☆ Lady Hawk
Lenni ☆ Leo ☆ Lexus ☆ Lucy ☆ Madison ☆ Maedchen ☆ Magic
Manieto ☆ Marisol ☆ Mars ☆ Martin ☆ Matthew ☆ Max ☆ Mozart
Mystic ☆ Nike ☆ Noah ☆ Oakie ☆ Orca ☆ Pablo ☆ Pascal
Patience ☆ Peter ☆ Petunia ☆ Philip ☆ Picasso ☆ Pockets ☆ Polliana
Pongo ☆ Princess ☆ Quincey ☆ Rachel ☆ Remmy ☆ Renaissance
Revel ☆ Rex ☆ Rio ☆ Risha ☆ Risky ☆ Rocky ☆ Romeo ☆ Rosie
Ruby ☆ Rudy ☆ Rufusi ☆ Sailor ☆ Sassy ☆ Schatzie ☆ Serafin
Smoke ☆ Solo ☆ Sonny ☆ Southern Comfort ☆ Sparkie ☆ Squirrel
Star ☆ Steven ☆ Superstition (Stitch) ☆ Surprise ☆ Susie ☆ Tarim
Teddy ☆ Teddy ☆ Tempi ☆ Texas ☆ Thoratio ☆ Thoren ☆ Tia
Tiny ☆ Tommy ☆ Trebose ☆ Tucker ☆ Ulena ☆ Utah ☆ Valentino
Van Gogh ☆ Versace ☆ Vin Diesel ☆ Wesley ☆ Whintey ☆ Windale
Xico ☆ Yang ☆ Yankie ☆ Yo Yo ☆ Zedair ☆ Zeloquent (Zealous)
Zepher ☆ Zorro ☆ Zorro

Abby ☆ Becky ☆ Benjamin ☆ Buck ☆ Clover ☆ Dolly ☆ EG ☆ Faust
Irish ☆ Jewel ☆ Kitten ☆ Lady ☆ Mort ☆ Pluto ☆ Poco Grande
(Gitano) ☆ Port ☆ Red ☆ Rejoice ☆ Scotty ☆ Sir William ☆ Tam
Tex ☆ Tudor

Akkie ☆ Andy ☆ Angel ☆ Arielle ☆ Art ☆ Bandy ☆ Beau
Beauty ☆ Beth ☆ Bow ☆ Buddy ☆ Cadbury ☆ Candyman ☆ Cat
Colty ☆ Computer ☆ Cosmo ☆ Cricket ☆ Crimson ☆ Daily
Dijou ☆ Dream Weaver ☆ Eli ☆ Excalibur ☆ Fame ☆ Filly ☆ Flair
Fredericktown (Freddie) ☆ Frisco Kid ☆ Gabriel ☆ Gitano ☆ Gustav
Happy ☆ Hombre ☆ In Style ☆ Genevieve ☆ John Henri ☆ Jubilee
Jude ☆ Judy ☆ Kass ☆ Lady ☆ Launching Pad ☆ Magic ☆ Major
Maus ☆ May Day ☆ Meddly ☆ Mic ☆ Mystic ☆ Nahli ☆ Newton
Oz ☆ Pearl ☆ Pietee ☆ Pinky ☆ Prayer ☆ Rafaele ☆ Ready Kilowatt
Rocky ☆ Saint ☆ Sandy ☆ Santikah ☆ Sarah ☆ See Squaw ☆ Sissie
Sophie ☆ Storm ☆ Sugar ☆ Sweetie ☆ TC ☆ Tim ☆ Toby
Toccata ☆ Tory ☆ Ty ☆ Virgil ☆ Umbra

from the
Horse's Mouth

from the
Horse's Mouth

A Horseman's Notes II

ERIK HERBERMANN

CORE PUBLISHING

This revised and expanded second edition published in the USA in 2015 by
Core Publishing
P.O. Box 3407
Crofton, MD 21114-0407

First published in the USA as *A Horseman's Notes* by
Core Publishing in 2003

ISBN 978 0 9723875 2 1

Library of Congress Control Number: 2014921167

Edited by Jane Lake
Page design by Paul Saunders

Printed in the USA by Taylor Specialty Books, Dallas, TX 75235

In dedication to furthering equestrian ideals
based on the nature of the horse.

Contents

Acknowledgments

In Gratitude to my Equine Teachers

A list of names of the many dear horses whom I have had the privilege of working with and learning from over the years have been placed – like two bookends – on the endpapers of this volume.

Beginning on the left front endpaper are the names of the horses who were present at the Reitinstitut Egon von Neindorff during the 30-plus years I annually attended the school – I had the honour of personally riding and learning from about eighty percent of the horses mentioned.

On the remainder of the front and back endpapers are the names of horses – some few of whom I owned and trained – but most of whom belonged to my students, on who they took lessons. Some names represent brief encounters, others long, rich relationships which lasted over decades. From the very first to the very last name mentioned, without exception, each horse has enriched my insight and appreciation of their generous and noble spirit. And collectively they have reconfirmed in me the solemn value of the observations made about their nature by the old Masters.

I am deeply grateful to all these marvelous creatures. Their quiet, true voice is inextricably interwoven throughout the pages of this book. This list of names is continually being supplemented and updated; it is incomplete.

In Gratitude to my Human Teachers

The vast canvas of horsemanship is truly a living, collective work compiled and refined over the centuries by many dedicated horsemen. Riding would not be what it is today without our being able to stand on their shoulders. Their contribution of astute, detailed observations about the horse's nature continues to guide us to this very day and are universally accepted as the back-bone of any worthwhile riding. The information in this book is no exception. It, too, is inescapably based on that solid foundation. Illustrations of those Masters whom I personally value most highly are included in this book, and their literary works are mentioned in the recommended reading list at the back. We owe them a sincere debt of gratitude for their pioneering work in this field.

Here I wish to acknowledge and express my thanks to those who have contributed to my equestrian education and to my personal life.

On the equestrian front, in chronological order, are: Walter Thiessen, Heidi Hannibal, Monty Smith, and Dietrich von Hopffgarten.

It was a privilege to have been taught by Mrs. Patricia Salt, FBHS, (1925–2011) when I first started serious study of horsemanship. She herself was a consummate equestrian who became a Fellow of the British Horse Society at the age of 21. Because of her extraordinary talent, she was one of the first female pupils to be accepted at the Spanish Riding School. Among her teachers there were Chief Rider Ernst Lindenbauer, Col. Hans Handler and Richard L. Wätjen.

I am particularly deeply indebted to Herr Egon von Neindorff (1923–2004), from whom I have gained the practical foundation on which I have built my equestrian experiences. I worked with Herr von Neindorff on a regular basis for 33 years, attending his school for several months each winter until his death in 2004. It was an exceptionally rich education to have worked under the guidance of this talented Master – a genius on horseback and dedicated teacher. For more than 50 years, Egon von Neindorff staunchly upheld classical teachings. And though his school and teaching were indeed exclusive – his doors were always open; and his horses and his teaching were available to literally anyone who wanted to come. His school presented a unique opportunity through which he was able to influence a broad cross-section of riders from around the world during his lifetime of dedicated service to horsemanship.

School horse Alea, Rumanian gelding, Levade with Egon von Neindorff (2002). Rider, Verena Geiger. Photo, Arnd Bronkhorst.

It is with fond appreciation that I remember my dear friend Dan Aharoni. Through his assistance *The Dressage Formula* was first published by J. A. Allen. The horse world owes Mr. Joseph A. Allen (1910–2001) much for his invaluable contribution of publishing fine equestrian literature during the 75 years in which he managed his company.

On the personal front, I wish first to express special thanks to my beloved wife, companion and friend, Erika, for her help with illustrations and for her endless patience, support and understanding during the time I was working on this book. Next, I feel deeply grateful to have been assisted by so many fine souls during my life, beginning with my beloved parents, Elizabeth and Joseph, and some extraordinary school teachers, Mr. Garnet A. (Tony) Parr, and Fr. John Hodgins – not to mention my appreciation for all I have gained from the many students whom I have had the privilege of teaching over the years.

A special thanks to Susan Dummit and John Pullen (1938–2004) for contributing insightful feedback on the manuscript of the *first* edition of *A Horseman's Notes*. The Buddha anecdote by Anthony de Mello was contributed by Jane Skiba; permission to use that quote was granted by Scott Reeves. Several other excerpts are from Jane Skiba's marvelous collection of philosophical quotes *Res ipsa loquitur.* These are located in sections 2.0, 4.9, 4.89b, 6.23, 7.4, 11.21, 11.29, 14.1. The quote from Epictetus was contributed by Marcia Koren. Many thanks to Judith Rakers for permission to use a quote from her interview with Frank Elstner on the German TV program *Menschen der Woche* (*People of the Week*).

Photo and illustration credits

My thanks for permission to reproduce photos and illustrations go to the following:

- *Cheval gris pommelé*, oil painting by Théodore Géricault (1791–1824), private collection, by permission of The Bridgeman Art Library International, London, New York, Paris.
- *Tête de Cheval blanc*, oil painting by Théodore Géricault (1791–1824), by permission of Musée de Louvre, Paris.
- Sketches by Ludwig Koch are from his book *Die Reitkunst im Bilde*, 1928, Vienna (reissued by George Olms Verlag AG., Hildesheim, Germany). Permission granted by Herr T. Brandner, Österreichische Campangereitergesellschaft, Vienna, Austria. Generous assistance given by Frau Christiane Busch, Olms Verlag AG., and by the Director of the Spanish Riding School, Dr. Jaromir Oulehla.
- The watercolour of school horse *Riffa*; the tempera painting of *The Red Horse*; and the oil painting of *The Appaloosa* were created by Karlsruhe artist Monika Bartsch and reproduced with her permission. She also produced the pen and ink line drawings for the two-track work in Chapter 10.
- The photo of Liselotte Linsenhoff, medium trot, on thoroughbred horse Monarchist, reproduced with permission of her daughter Ann Kathrin Linsenhoff.
- The cover photo of Lusitano stallion Orion, reproduced with permission of the owner Frau Andrea Klohe. Photo by Valentina Goeck.
- The before-and-after photos of Royal Doulton, used with permission of owner Kathy Fessler. Photo by Kemra Martin Arias.
- Photo of half-pass (travers), right, on Hanoverian mare Jacqueline; the photo of piaffe on Andalusian stallion Juca (taken by Prof. U. Schnitzer); the extended trot photo; the levade photo of Alea (taken by Arnd Bronkhorst 2002), reproduced by permission of Egon von Neindorff (2002).
- Permission for reproduction of Waldemar Seunig riding passage, granted by Frau Beatrix Zurek, representing the Seunig family.

- Photo of Johann Meixner in the levade, by permission of the Director of the Spanish Riding School, Dr. Jaromir Oulehla.
- The engraving of Pluvinel instructing the king from *Le Maneige Royal*, and the engraving from *School of Horsemanship*, François Robichon de la Guérinière, by permission of Caroline Burt (First Edition) and Lesley Gowers (Second Edition), J. A. Allen publishers, an imprint of Robert Hale Ltd., London.
- Illustration of Andalusian stallion Banbury Sampson, by permission of Sally Cleaver.
- The photos of Gitano and Pluto by permission of the owner Margot Huelke. Photos by Alston Wolf.
- Photo of Jiji Mellon, jumping Dante, reproduced with her permission. Photo taken by Lawrence.
- Photo of blacksmith, Herr Glaser (taken by Dieter Schuchmann), private photo collection by permission of Frau Erika Luy and Herr Fritz Luy.
- The photographs of the author on Barty were taken by George A. Ross.
- The Hubble Space Telescope image # 9821a1, of barrel-spiral galaxy NG4314. Reproduced by permission of NASA and The Hubble Heritage Team: Space Telescope Science Institute (STScI), and The Association of Universities for Research in Astronomy, Inc., (AURA). Further acknowledgment for assistance to Christopher J. Conselice (U. Wisconsin, STScI). My thanks to Janet Hurst for her assistance acquiring the images.

My special thanks and appreciation to Jane Lake, the editor; and to Paul Saunders, the designer, for having taken such care to help produce this book so beautifully.

Preface

THIS NEW VOLUME IS A completely revised and expanded edition of its predecessor. It has been named *From the Horse's Mouth* because of my conviction that excellence in horsemanship can develop reliably only when we earnestly strive to listen to the horses for their approval of our interaction with them. In addition, this title expresses an essential truth, that every word in this book comes straight from my heart; 'from the horse's mouth', so to speak.

For those who have known me as a teacher over the past 40-plus years, know that my writings are not mere words to me. They reflect my soul's very direction which I strive to live – and encourage my students to live – with every ounce of my energy and with unwavering reverence for the horse. The very foundation on which my equestrian endeavors have always rested, is that the horse's nature should ever prevail as our indisputable, empirical guide – decidedly more important than any of our human opinions. It is therefore my dearest wish that the light of the horse's 'wordless words' – which I have passionately sought and learned to cherish over the years – will somehow shine through the text of these pages.

While fully embracing the reality that the horse's nature is constant and that the equestrian principles remain firmly anchored in Natural Law, the way in which to describe our approach to the horse – or how to improve ourselves relative to the task – is broad indeed. Accordingly, with this book I wish to share the many improved descriptions, explanations and insights I have gained during the intervening years of teaching since the first edition of *A Horseman's Notes* appeared in 2003. This has resulted in new chapters and new or rewritten material to be included. Much of the text is presented in short, subtitled paragraphs, each with its own number. This acts as a cross-reference for finding related material throughout the book. The first number before the period indicates the chapter; the number after the period indicates the section. Quick searching is also made easy by way of the highly-detailed index which contains well over a thousand entries.

The contents of this volume deals with a broad spectrum of practical, technical details about the seat, position, aiding, and exercises. Two-track work is also more thoroughly addressed. However, in light of the horse's remarkable sensitivity to our unspoken, underlying attitudes, many concepts are interwoven throughout the text which underscore the relevance of knowing how to direct our thoughts, intentions and feelings beneficially towards the horse. This all ties in to my belief that the inherent requirements of riding finds its home deeply rooted in the innermost laws of the universe, of which we and the horses are an inseparable part. Because of this, subject matter has been included which goes beyond the purely equestrian.

If we look at this subject in sober light, I feel we can not help but conclude that the quality of our work depends not so much on how many exercises or movements we can 'make' a horse do but, rather, it is reflected in the quality and worthiness of our interaction with our four-legged friends, whose nature should ever remain our Holy Grail – pure and unsullied. Let us then be inspired by these delightful creatures. And, if we have not already done so, let us resolve to have a change of heart away from all that is unfriendly or discordant; and strive to follow a higher calling – one befitting the honour both the horse and horsemanship deserve. In this way we can give wings to our collective work and become part of a renaissance of excellence in this our beloved art and science. Surely the success of this rests entirely in our own hands, each and every one of us – who will we choose to serve?

It is my most sincere wish that the thoughts expressed between these covers may engender the desire to cultivate beautiful horsemanship.

ERIK HERBERMANN
Karlsruhe, 2015

Enter the sanctuary of the horse
ever with honour and respect

Cheval gris pommelé. *Théodore Géricault (1791–1824). Private collection. The Bridgeman Art Library International Ltd., London/New York/Paris.*

The Illustrations

THE AIM IN CHOOSING illustrations for this book has been to present some of the finest examples of horsemanship which portray both technical and philosophical excellence in the classical tradition. Among the many wonderful examples are the engravings of Pluvinel's and de la Guérinière's work; Ludwig Koch's exquisite line drawings of work he observed at the old (pre 1928) Spanish Riding School; the vibrant paintings of Théodore Géricault; artwork by the talented present-day artist, Monika Bartsch; Olympic-level riding represented in a photo of Frau Liselott Linsenhoff on Monarchist. In addition, many fine photographs of the old Masters also grace the pages of this book – Johann Meixner, Ernst Lindenbauer, Waldemar Seunig, Richard Wätjen, and Egon von Neindorff. Finally, numerous line drawings are also included depicting two-track exercises.

In contrast to the considerable difficulty of finding pictures of such perfection, it was certainly easy enough to find examples of not-so-perfect work – they were right there in my personal photo collection.

Illustrations of the horse without rider are also included. I believe that our observation of horses at liberty, demonstrating their phenomenal natural capacity while out at play, would have to be among the central pillars in our arsenal to help keep our perceptions and our work in the saddle on a viable, nature-oriented path as much as possible.

When first seeing Théodore Géricault's painting *Cheval gris pommelé*, see opposite, one may feel that it is just an artist's exaggerated impression. Yet, I am almost certain it is not, having witnessed one particular young Arab stallion who would occasionally do picture-perfect levades in his stall with deeply bent haunches, hocks barely inches off the ground, as the mares were led past his stall on their way out to pasture in the morning. He would, in fact, hop around, doing a sort of turn on the haunches in the levade, apparently wanting to face the mares as they came and went by. Another remarkable instance was that of an Appaloosa gelding. When just turned out, he would occasionally canter up a steep slope to a knoll at the top of his paddock, and perform two or three absolutely classical caprioles in succession. I have often regretted not having captured these incidents on camera.

With these experiences in mind, to me it is by no means far-fetched that a horse would do a canter pirouette with deeply bent haunches while at liberty. Yet, it is understandable that it may seem like nothing but fantasy to those who have never seen fine riding in which the horse's deeply bent haunches turn into slow, elastic pistons, combining awesome power with deceptive ease, while the horse's mind, though eager, remains entirely calm.

One may similarly wish to dismiss the Ludwig Koch sketches as being merely a collection of idealized artistic expressions. But we are fortunate to have several excellent touchstones to help authenticate Koch's incisive observations. One photograph in particular of the stallion Banbury Sampson at liberty, see page 134, demonstrates the beauty and harmony of balanced forwardness with deeply engaged hindquarters, and perfect 'relative erection' of his forehand, with his poll at the highest point and face ahead of the vertical. Though full of energy, he is wonderfully calm and supple. These very uphill qualities radiate unambiguously from Koch's depictions of the Spanish Riding School's work.

Before continuing, I must briefly digress to give heartfelt thanks to all those horsemen, past or present, who have remained true to their calling as custodians of the equestrian art, and who, because they have not sold their souls for financial gains or personal glory, have been able to leave us with their illuminating and inspiring examples. For instance, we have the magnificent photograph of Oberbereiter Ernst Lindenbauer, page 4, showing us that it is possible to achieve such independent, uphill beauty in the horse under saddle. We can readily compare this with identical attributes in the Koch sketch, see page 13. Similar correlations can be seen between Koch's depiction of the levade, page 24, and the photograph of Oberbereiter Johann Meixner's levade, see page 42. In all these works the artists have clearly recreated an admirably precise image of exactly what they saw.

In summarizing, much can be gained when the time is taken to absorb quietly and patiently the essence these illustrations emanate – to reignite an awareness and interest in those vitally important details of our equestrian science and art, so that these qualities will appear not only in photos and artworks from a bygone era, but may become a living truth once more in the daily practice of present-day riders.

View Video of the old Spanish Riding School (circa *1935)*

To view rare **black and white** film of riding at the *old* Spanish Riding School, and see horses going beautifully uphill, with deeply bent haunches – **Google** the following sentence:

Vienna. I cavallerizzi di un'antica scuola di equitazione si esibiscono in passi classici di alta – YouTube

Noteworthy points in the video:

- The clearly-lowered haunches, producing the characteristic uphill quality in the horses throughout the ride. Such beautiful, correct work is extremely rare these days.
- The old standard: 'two-thirds of the horse in front of the rider, one-third behind' – is explicitly demonstrated.
- The gaits are smooth, powerful, forward and pure. They float elastically. There is no sign of unwanted tense 'hovering' in the collected gaits.
- The riders' seats are absolutely quiet because they are being carried forward on the horse's balanced, supple, carrying backs.

Ernst Lindenbauer, Oberberreiter at the Spanish Riding School. Working canter right. Note the beautiful uphill attitude originating from the deeply bent hindquarters. Two-thirds of the horse in front of the rider, one-third behind. Absolute perfection.

CHAPTER I

Overture to Horsemanship

1.1 What could possibly be more sublime – intoxicating, really – than experiencing those exquisite moments of harmony with the horse, when we feel effortlessly buoyed-up on the full, elastic waves of his carrying back and sense the awesome power, the delightful eagerness of this sensitive creature beneath us.

1.2 Here a little, there a little, serendipitously at first, glimpses of such fine experiences begin to occur to us, usually changing forever our view of what a true partnership with the horse could be like. In fact, the momentousness of those apparently small happenings seems to leave us with an irrational, bone-dry thirst for experiencing those glorious moments again. It is as though some irresistible force were compelling us inexorably to search for that elusive sanctuary of oneness – beckoning like the serene beauty of an emerald lake hidden somewhere deep within the mountains of our being.

1.3 In truth, the emerald lake represents a state of being whole, a merging with the deepest essence of the horse. When we are there, however briefly, we are it, and it is us. Likewise, when we are not there, that too, at that moment, is us ...

1.4 On the other hand, the pathway to the emerald lake represents the process, the detailed, conscious journey towards that state. It is the living principle, the living law of the horse that we must come to know and follow with passionate certainty if we are to succeed in our pilgrimage. Not one false cell of our being will slip surreptitiously past the gatekeeper. In fact, the path is firmly barred to those who seek primarily for their own ends. Only when the horse is fully taken into account as a highly respected partner in the cause – his needs wholly and faithfully met – are the legitimate avenues opened, and can the metamorphosis of two-becoming-one begin to occur.

1.5 Reaching the emerald lake is an aspiration which taxes every aspect of our being: body, mind, and spirit. It is a journey which embodies consummate joy as it gives us the opportunity to develop and experience the potency and richness of our talents. And, with equal vigour, it confronts us with the exacting, prickly challenges of gaining control over our body, and to brave the less well-developed aspects of our spiritual being. Though it is at times a daunting and troublesome process, when it is taken on with clarity and enduring courage, it becomes immensely rewarding – especially as we begin to sense its far-reaching, benign undertones wafting like a gentle, healing fragrance into every corner of our lives.

The Red Horse. *Monika Bartsch. Tempera painting on cotton cloth, 1988. 180 x 180 cm.*

CHAPTER II

In the Garden of Heart and Mind

He to whom Nature begins to reveal her open secrets will feel an irresistible yearning for her most worthy interpreter, art.

WOLFGANG GOETHE

Introduction

2.0 In the quest to improve our riding, the technicalities are often given the lion's share of attention as compared to the philosophical considerations. Of course, no one would deny the importance of technique, or that actions speak louder than words. Nor would anyone dispute that riding entails the joy of sitting on a horse, learning how to communicate with and guide him benevolently. But it must be equally clear that actions can be entirely unproductive, inappropriate or even harmful unless they are well directed by wisdom, intelligent consideration and wholesome attitudes. Surely, horsemanship is no more than a relatively crude undertaking in the absence of an evolved, integrated philosophy. We could view a sound ideology as the fertile soil in which the seeds of technique are able to sprout and take root, giving harmony between horse and rider a greater opportunity to unfold.

The following points explore these elements in greater detail.

2
2.1

From the heart

2.1 Enduring respect, love and passion for horses are the mainstays of our equestrian art. These do not originate from the intellect but, as with genuine friendship, they are an outpouring of the human heart. Horses love to feel loved, to sense we think highly of them: that they are important to us. They notice especially when we show enjoyment and appreciation for their responsiveness. It is precisely these heartfelt qualities that awaken the horse's childlike enthusiasm to show us they know what we want and are eager to fulfil our wishes.

They can read

2.2 Horses have a remarkable talent for reading our hearts, our innermost motives. Often they respond more to the quality of our attitudes and intentions than our actions. This can be readily seen in horses who patiently take care of tiny children or awkward beginners. Though they may be unbalanced and end up accidentally tugging and pulling on the reins, even quite roughly, the horses sense no harm is meant and are unconcerned about it. This emphasizes the value of having sincere goodwill towards our equine partner and how that can notably ease the task of learning to ride.

Power of immanent thinking

2.3 Irrespective of the circumstances, or the level of talent, the rider is the leader of the equestrian partnership. An essential aspect of leadership entails the ability to think immanently. This means we can think and plan ahead without these thoughts being disclosed in any way – that is, not until we are ready to tell the horse about our intentions. In other words, preparation is good, but don't tell your horse what you are preparing him for, nor why a certain exercise is being done – just do it! This does not mean horses should be surprised or ambushed. Rather, immanent thinking helps diminish the horse's anticipation and offering unwanted or premature responses. Here also, the power of apparently ignoring everything we don't want, while patiently and persistently showing the horse what we do want, is central to success. The value of immanent thinking can further be appreciated when we observe inexperienced riders who run into all manner of difficulty because they are unable to keep the thought 'canter' to themselves, or are unable to remain serene and relaxed when the horse gets nervous.

It is our task

2.4 When running into difficulties, riders at times feel as though horses are set on doing them in. Yet, if we wish to progress, it is important to accept that the task of horsemanship lies entirely with the rider to become more equine, and not for the horse to become human. When this view is embraced and lived, a delightful discovery soon becomes evident that the creatures feel neither the need nor desire to outwit the rider, and usually come more than halfway to respond to any reasonable requests (**4.18**).

Two 'positions'

2.5 A correct physical 'position' which is in harmony with the laws of physics is indispensable to allow essential energy patterns to flow through our own and the horse's body. So too, a sound mental 'position' – constructive, wholesome, benign thinking – enables *that* to flow through and strengthen all our endeavours. Horses innately respect and willingly follow good attitudes and positive, harmonious thought power.

Take care …

2.6 Conversely, our negative thinking easily disturbs the horse and results in distrust, fear and tension. Without wanting to dwell unduly on such matters, I believe it is worthwhile to look briefly at the most common personal obstacles to success in horsemanship:

- **on the aggressive side**: unfitting ambitions, immoderate requests, arrogance, anger, intimidation, fault-finding; being inconsiderate, unkind, impatient, reproachful, bearing grudges, resentment, kindling vengeance.

- **on the timid side:** being irresolute, hesitant, indecisive, self-effacing, fearful, lacking control over the emotions.

Note Even if we might be angry or frustrated only with ourselves, horses are unable to discern that it is not directed at them. They sense and reflect our anger or fear irrespective of to whom or at what it is aimed. To succeed at horsemanship it is essential to learn to control our attitudes, emotions and thinking (**4.44, 12.6**).

Character

2.7 It takes strength of character and solid self-confidence to row against the stream of popular trends or outward appearances, and to follow our heart towards things of deeper value, those rooted in natural principle instead. For, if we are not constantly vigilant, any one of us can all too readily be driven by our unruly egos, self-serving ambitions, or be seduced by peer pressure, or by financial, political and social considerations. The horse is seldom well served by these and usually suffers because of them.

About ideals

2.8 It is indeed helpful to our progress to establish ideals both in riding and in our lives. Contrary to what one might think, ideals are not some form of wishful thinking, nor are they even remotely impractical. Rather, they are essential beacons which help us draw our desires ever upward. This keeps our activities on a valid course and extends our efforts beyond that which we might ordinarily do. Short-term ideals are those by which we test ourselves on a daily, weekly, or monthly basis. Long-term ideals could well serve us for many years, if not a lifetime. Interestingly, the establishing of ideals is a uniquely personal matter. They are wholly dependent on our individual outlook and level of awareness at any given stage of our unfolding. It is therefore important to reset ideals every now and then as new horizons of insight develop through the knowledge and experience we gain over time. In this way, through our ideals we have the ongoing opportunity to define and express our ever-evolving vision of the excellence we hope to manifest in our riding and in our lives (11.35, 11.43, 12.3, 14.4).

Who do we follow?

2.9 In competition we find out if a judge likes our work, or if we are better than other riders. In the spirit of classical horsemanship, however, we seek to determine whether the horses approve of our interaction with them, and hold ourselves up to the light of their innocent and unassailable truths (11.28, 11.29, 11.31–11.33).

Ludwig Koch. A spirited, shortened working canter left. Compare with photo on page 4.

The horse's voice

2.10 In light of this, the human judge's opinion could only be considered of value if it faithfully listens to and represents the horses' 'voice'. Judging therefore bears exceptional responsibility, especially considering the creatures are entirely at our mercy. Their views are often expressed subtly and in a 'language' which requires much time and effort on our part to comprehend. Because of this the horse's 'messages' can easily be dismissed by our intellect or overruled by unfitting ambitions. Thus, if we wish to grow ever more harmonious with them, it is vital to work strictly within the horses' natural capacities – to guide without violating their joyful spirit and, through intelligent gymnastic work, help form the raw gold of their physical talents into a lovely jewel.[1]

The delicate rays of truth

2.11 The clarity of vision needed to carry out such guardianship develops gradually. It requires years of honest searching in the saddle, based on singular, incorruptible loyalty to the horse. Through such hard-won experience our sensitivity is awakened and the delicate rays of the horse's truth gradually dawn in our consciousness. In this way it becomes ever more clear how, through our benign interaction, the creatures become encircled in a state of wellbeing which unlocks the treasure of their generosity to us. And how, through the struggle to fulfil our equestrian task, we are enriched by having to grow beyond ourselves.

Der Kluge gibt nach (He who is wise yields)

2.12 It is up to us to initiate harmonious resolutions to any negative occurrences. The horses do not know how to do so, and tend to continue to resist (that which they perceive to be *our* resistance against them) until we help them out of their cul-de-sac by dissolving the resistance in ourselves first. In this way we give them nothing to be against in the first place (For ways of how to defuse tensions see **4.27, 4.79, 4.80, 5.9, 5.31, 6.12, 6.14, 6.28, 6.35–6.37, 7.7, 7.8**).

It is holy

2.13a For the horseman the cultivation of willing participation is a sacred bond. Submission is equestrian bankruptcy. Willing participation is a joyful contribution based on trust and understanding which the horse gradually gains from a quiet, patient, consistent

1 See the three-point guideline in 7.0 the introduction to Chapter VII, page 119.

routine. Submission is based on coercion which usually leads either to horses' soulless obedience, or outright protest. It would be remiss, however, not to mention – and unrealistic to ignore or deny – that on rare occasion we may briefly need to use stronger or sharper aiding to clarify a point or to assert our leadership. But exactly then, contrary to what one might think, it takes enormous finesse to do that well and can succeed only when based on the cornerstone of benevolence and respect towards the horse (**4.9**).

The golden middle ground

2.13b As with virtually any subject, extremes are unhelpful. Neither the faint-heart rider, or the overly-conscientious, though well-meaning soul – nor the aggressive, disrespectful, insensitive individual – will succeed in the task of horsemanship. Besides the obvious need for equestrian skill and understanding based on adequate experience, the finest leadership is a state in which inner strength, confidence and purposefulness is merged with compassion, gentleness and patience (**4.89a, b, c**).

'Harmony'?

2.14 What kind of harmony would ensue if we were to command our human partner, 'I *order* you to dance with me!' Is it really all that different if we wish to dance with horses without respectfully inviting and encouraging their willing participation?

Wisdom

2.15 That which the ancients tell us is surely worthy of note: 'Amongst those whom thou dost call thy friends and thine enemies, there is not one iota of difference'.[2] With these words, are they not trying to help us see that we can either validate and enrich, or undermine and make destructive, our relationships and experiences, depending almost entirely on how we approach the creatures, people or circumstances we meet?

2 The Teachings of Osiris. Also implied in Luke 6:26–42.

Un-force-able

2.16 Willing participation is indisputably a gift from the horse. The very core of fine horsemanship ultimately rests on the horse's free choice to *allow* us in to the centre of his being. This can not be forced. It can only be given space to blossom through being respectful and earning trust. In other words, being fair and consistent in our requests and having a pure heart with benign intentions gives this 'opening up' of the horse's being to our leadership the greater chance of occurring. *Any* forcing is an offence against the spirit of the horse and diametrically opposes willing participation.

Note See sections **4.9**, **4.42**, **4.43b**, **4.44f**, about appreciating the difference between fair and suitable use of stick and spurs during tuning, and that which would be considered unacceptable 'forcing'. Also see Introduction **6.0**, which clarifies why horses by nature do not expend more energy than absolutely necessary; and therefore the importance of the rider's responsibility for exciting forward energy during riding.

Fitness of another kind

2.17 What makes a tree strong but to endure frost, drought, heat, and storms! If we wish to take up the challenge, horsemanship affords us plenty of opportunity through which our character, our being, our soul can grow ever more resilient and sound.

Habits

2.18 Only through determined effort, applied over extended periods, are good habits formed and do unwanted traits gradually atrophy through disuse.

No sweepstakes

2.19 Riding is not a lottery. Through developing good habits we can paint the winning numbers on the equestrian lottery balls ourselves – and that at any time we wish.

Our 'luck'

2.20 It is indeed humbling for us as we begin to see the actual measure of our being, relative to the enormity of all existence, and realize we only ever *re*discover laws, truths and principles by which the universe has already operated since the birth of time. Surely an inexpressible feeling of relief and gratitude washes over us as we become aware of the grace accorded us by Universal Law which abides patiently and steadily, with or without our understanding or approval. Even our misperceptions and errors are charitably endured as we struggle to find understanding and harmony with Nature's unerring ways. Isn't it exactly this simple, honest forbearance – the healing and forgiveness of Nature – which is exemplified by horses when they unfailingly go well the moment we ride well, even after years of misapplied and confused attempts?

Ludwig Koch. Collected walk. Note the clear, balanced 'oneness', and the poll-high head position of the horse which portrays the inner validity of the work.

Finding truth

2.21 In the fullness of their unselfconscious glory, the dear horses help us find truth because they are pure, guileless reflections of it. Though words may fail to describe it, we sense truth as a gut feeling, a reflection we recognize intuitively as it reverberates on the soundboard of our soul. When in our struggles we no longer seem to know which way to go, we can find solace in giving ourselves patiently to the wisdom of Nature. This may be compared to writing a poem when the one holding the pen yields and becomes a mere instrument – a scribe – sitting at the foot stool of truth that begs to be told, and faithfully writes that truth without interfering with it – whether it appears as 'words' of beauty flowing from the saddle, or as holy writ penned upon paper.

An expert

2.22 Who is an expert in any field, but one who has come to understand the Natural Laws on which the materials with which they work are based. The deeper the understanding of those laws and the closer one cooperates with them, the finer the product. In horsemanship the horse is our *living* medium, our *living* canvas with whom we can strive to 'paint' glorious, elastic dances.

A narrow path

2.23 Surely then, developing the power of observation of the Laws of Nature as they are expressed in the horse, and striving to cooperate with them, is essential if we wish to develop fine horsemanship. It is the narrow path to be followed if we wish to become one with those invisible principles concealed within the visible world around us. That which is most important, however, is not only the effort we expend and the heart with which we approach this subject but, above all, that we develop our understanding and skills in such a way that we cause minimal adverse effects on the horses while our education is in process.

The bottom line

2.24 When all is said and done, I believe the only thing that truly counts will be what residue, beneficial or ruinous, our actions and efforts will have left on the souls of those around us, and on the creatures with whom we have dealt during our lives.

Egon von Neindorff on Hanoverian mare Jacqueline; travers (half-pass) right. Beautiful harmony and dynamic 'straightness', based on the excellence of the rider's position and attitudes.

CHAPTER III

The Physical Spectrum

Monsieur de Pluvinel always sits in the same posture, up straight, whether he is putting the horse into the airs or at the walk; and I have often heard him say that for a Horseman to be graceful, he must never, when making a horse perform, move, except to raise very gently the arm up and down, back and forth, to make the switch whistle.

MONSIEUR LE GRAND[1]

Introduction

3.0 The rider's physical seat and position comprises not only the obvious external form, but also encompasses the full gamut of intangible attitudes which are inseparable from, and governed by, the mental 'position'. The physical follows the spiritual. Thus, the body's outer appearance can reliably mirror the degree of understanding and development of our entire equestrian proficiency. The qualities of patience, modesty and kindness, for example, radiate from the physical as an ineffable serenity and gracefulness; and the simple economy of elegance exists only when significant levels of physical and spiritual harmony have been achieved within the rider. These characteristics are implicitly

1 From *Le Maneige Royal*, Pluvinel. p24. J.A. Allen & Co. Ltd., 1969. English translation by Hilda Nelson, 1989

unfalsifiable, and can not help but spill over to reflect their likeness in the horse.

Though this chapter inevitably deals with technical elements of body posture, nevertheless, numerous points describe attitudes, feelings or just 'ways of thinking' rather than necessarily implying the need for overt physical adjustments. These seemingly subtle changes in outlook have surprisingly large effects on the horse, and become ever more marked as the rider gains better control over basic physical position.

For the sake of analysis, many position attributes are discussed separately. It is important, however, to avoid isolating these points. Rather, they should be seen as an integral part of a larger system which we should constantly strive to combine harmoniously. The reason for making any position adjustments in the rider should always have a practical purpose for making viable changes in the horse's way of going.

Part I · Mind Over Body

Tensions

3.1 For both horse and rider, the state of mind directly affects the state of the body. Mental calmness brings physical relaxation. The rider's own mental calmness is indispensable to soothe and encourage the horse's mental calmness. Furthermore, without the rider's calmness, essential serenity can not exist. Without serenity we can not feel. Without feeling we can not participate. Without participation a harmonious dance with the horse is not possible. For ways to calm the horse's physical and mental tensions, refer to 4.79, 4.83, 6.12, 6.28, 6.33, 6.35–6.37, 7.7, 8.7.

Overcoming tensions

3.2 The rider's mental tension may be eased through breathing exercises, meditation and visualization aimed at gaining serenity, building self-confidence, patience and trust. Learning to make positive affirmations can be helpful in this regard, especially to overcome unwanted habits and fears.

Power of positive 'affirmations'

3.3 Being the leader of the partnership, it is unavoidable that we riders, by our very presence in the saddle, set the tone or ambience of the physical and psychological scene. Therefore, only through being steady, calm and non-reactionary can we help horses become calm, confident and non-reactionary to the many things in their environment that can make them jumpy – including a jumpy rider! Nevertheless, it is only natural for the rider to startle when horses startle. It is an involuntary, kneejerk reaction. There is no time to decide whether to react or not. Yet, it is absolutely crucial to learn to be unaffected by the horse's startling. To gain control over this we need to access our subconscious mind where habits dwell and involuntary reactions originate. This is where positive affirmations come to the rescue.

Power of invisible training

3.4 Using the above example, we can overcome such involuntary reactions by making, the following positive affirmation (in your own words): 'Next time I'll remain calm and relaxed'. We need to say these words to ourselves with quiet certainty – with absolute faith and expectancy. The next helpful thought is, 'I've got that now'; or 'I trust myself to remain calm' – as though it were already natural to be non-reactionary to such startling. We need to say the words *each time* the startling happens and be prepared for the long-haul. It may take fifty or sixty times for the good effects of positive affirmations to begin to show. Then, suddenly, like a miracle, on the sixty-first time, we will suddenly notice that we did not react when the horse startled! Presto! It worked!

Quiet determination

3.5 With positive affirmations, quiet, confident determination works best. To be avoided is the fist-slamming 'I *will* overcome this!' Or to make an affirmation with a negative statement, 'Next time my horse startles, I will *not* react!' Such concepts only entrench the unwanted, involuntary response more deeply. Needless to say, 'Oh, no, I did it again!'; or 'I'll never get this!', will really not help at all. To quote Jonathan Bach, from his book *Illusions*, 'Argue for your shortcomings and sure enough they are yours!'

Letting go

3.6 Some other ways to find mental serenity and physical relaxation are: 1) consciously and deliberately make our face, jaw and tongue slack, especially during aiding. 2) be aware of feeling the soles of our boots under our feet; 3) spread and wiggle our toes.

Living with the movement

3.7 Physical tensions can also be overcome by **movement** – warming up with some stretching exercises before mounting; or doing longeing exercises (on or off the longe); or thinking of dancing (boogieing) with the horse while riding. These are especially helpful ways to unlock shoulders, hip joints, knees and thighs (**3.16**).

Ludwig Koch. Levade. The pinnacle of balance, and ultimate elastic compression of the horse's hindquarters. Compare with photo page 42.

Good riding is breath-taking!

3.8 Unconscious holding of breath is another common symptom of inner tensions. This inevitably causes tension in the horse. (As one might imagine, carrying a 'non-breathing corpse' can frighten the wits out of a horse!).To gain relaxed breathing, it can be helpful to recite inwardly the following statements in time with the horse's stepping. At the walk (while breathing **in**): 'a hundred and twenty one'; (while breathing **out**): 'a hundred and twenty two', etc. At the trot: 'IN– 2 – 3 – 4'; 'OUT– 2 – 3 – 4'. At the canter: 'IN – 2 – 3'; 'OUT – 2 – 3' The numbers are counted in time with the strides of each respective gait. The number of strides for 'in' and 'out' can be adjusted to suit individual needs (**7.6a**).

Refreshingly free

3.9 To maintain suppleness and sensitivity over extended periods, it is best to think of refreshing the position instead of trying to hold it correctly. This can be as simple as thinking of 'breathing in, and breathing out' the position corrections; or we could 'fluff-up our feathers' every once in a while, and pretend we have just begun. These concepts provide us with a new start and help wash away staleness that may have seeped in from all our trying. By making a natural cycle in all we do, whether correcting ourselves or aiding the horse, we can avoid stiffness, tension and fatigue (**3.17**).

A balanced approach

3.10 Neither a strictly physical nor a purely intellectual approach to riding is effective. We need to develop a suitable balance between thinking and feeling.

Part II · Physical Adjustments

The influence of the position

An excellent position is like a beautiful, well-made instrument, ever prepared to be used for a delicate operation. It could be described as a zero or neutral position because it neither hinders nor influences the horse unless used deliberately. On the other hand, a poor position is like being 'in the red', because it impedes the horse's movement through awkwardness, tension, or involuntary movement of the rider. Like trying to do brain surgery with a garden hoe, the poor seat and position can not be used with the refinement needed to do excellent work.

Just a 'pole'

3.11 Think of the upper body resting on the seat as being a steady, balanced, vertical telephone pole. It is the essential constant under which – and relative to which – the horse learns to balance himself and work independently. The elastic quality of the spine could be compared to a riding stick, 'It has structure but is flexible' (Jayme).

Power of pillars

3.12 To gain accurate control over the weight in the seat bones, I use an analogy of having two imaginary pillars in the upper body, one on either side of the spine. Each pillar stands above its respective seat bone and we must strive to keep them both equal and viable. If one pillar is weak, it causes the shoulder to drop and the waist (hip) to collapse on that side. This weakens the entire aiding system and leads to poor control over alignment, balance and accuracy of school figures.

Making the 'X'

3.13 An effective way to become 'square' in the saddle (or to correct a collapsed hip/waist) is to make a living X through our body: stretch from the right heel (or hip) to the left shoulder, and from the left heel (or hip) to the right shoulder. Stretch back and forth alternately several times until we feel that the shoulders are even in height and square above the hips. Another concept for squaring up the hips, is to think of the legs as being an integral part of the hips. Then, from the waist up, the upper body must rise up independently and elegantly above the hips.

Energy = Water

3.14 Though we may be collapsing in only one hip (waist, pillar), it causes the seat to become entirely defunct. Why? Because it is no more possible to control the horse's energy with only one seat bone on the saddle, than to channel water with only one river bank. Having two equal seat bones on the saddle at all times, because of those two sound pillars, is the key to keeping the horse squarely under us, *laterally* well controlled between the seat bones. The legs and reins only become truly effective once evenness of the seat bones is established. Always remember: *Let yourself rest*!

Power of kneeling

3.15 The horse will not reach properly into the bridle on the side where the seat-bone energy is lagging or has dropped behind the knee. It is essential to keep the energy pattern of each seat bone constantly over the knee on its own side. This can be achieved by thinking of kneeling, which correctly opens the hip joint (i.e., the hip/thigh angle) and helps the knees to remain deep. The kneeling sensation is attained by:

- keeping the lower leg immediately behind the girth; do not pull it back and up!
- flattening the lower back;
- tucking the seat bones *elastically* and *gently* under (pelvic tilt) without shortening the front line (**9.23b**, **9.30b**);
- directing the seat bones forward into the front of the saddle (without leaning back);

– thinking of pressing the seat bones through the thighs over the horse's ears as you leave your knees and legs behind you. This also applies at the rising phase of the rising trot;

– thinking of sitting beyond the knees.

These points are mainly subtle thoughts, essences or mere energy patterns. Avoid any tightening of the seat muscles or using power or exaggerating. Again, we must keep in mind the most important basic seat and position principle: Always *let* yourself *rest* straight down in the deepest part of the saddle. Rest on the triangle. For more about the importance of the knee, see **4.29**, **4.82**.

Settling the seat

3.16 Experimenting with the following concepts at the walk for a few minutes at the beginning of the ride can help settle the seat bones better on the saddle and achieve a more independent seat. This may be found useful when there is no opportunity to be properly longed:

a) Repeatedly pick up the stirrups, then drop them again (five or six times in a row); this helps bring about relaxation and independent use of the lower leg during aiding.[2]

b) The feeling in the seat should remain steady, resting and the same whether we ride with or without stirrups.

c) When riding without stirrups we should alternate between either letting our toes dangle down, or raising them up gently (no more than 65 per cent to avoid tension); and deepen the heels (do not jam them down!) without the seat changing in its depth, steadiness or relaxation.

d) We should be able to raise and lower one leg at a time (keep the heel under the centre of the hip joint as you do so; i.e., do not lift the lower leg back and up), without causing tensions, changes in the position, squareness of the upper body/hips, or the steadiness and resting of the seat bones on the saddle.

2 Exercise contributed by Sue Terrall.

Both legs can also be raised simultaneously, but keep the lower back flat while doing so; this helps keep the seat bones pointing forward and it tones the stomach.

e) Because the hip joints, thighs, knees, and ankles are relaxed, the legs are able to hang relaxed and heavy or leaden.

f) We should be able to turn *only* the lower legs inward (without involving the thigh), until the feet are parallel to the horse's sides (not to be forced!); and/or gently raise only the toes up (a slight, invisible lightening-up of the ball of the foot or toe off the stirrup) while *letting* the heels relax more downward without losing that relaxed, heavy feeling in the legs.

g) We should be just as *resting* at the *rising* phase as we are at the sitting phase of the rising trot. The seat should feel the same and the horse should feel the same. We must not lose that steady, unified, balanced, relaxed, *resting* feeling.

h) Scissoring with the legs, or doing forward or backward 'bicycle pedaling' exercises with the legs are also useful adjuncts.

Front line

3.17 Acquiring an open front line is based on a soft, liberating attitude of the upper body. Think of 'laying open' the front line. *Allow* this to happen. Do not force it. Breathe in while imagining you are gently swinging open a pair of large French doors overlooking a meadow.

How to achieve a good front line?

3.18 Technically, an effective front line forms a capital **'D'**, when looking at the rider from the side. It is like a spinnaker on a sail boat, filled by a breeze from behind. It entails four distinct elements which are to be *gently* applied:

a) Raise the solar plexus (ribcage) *gently* up-and-back into the back of the collar, while simultaneously filling and stretching the nape of the neck into the back of the collar.

b) Allow the shoulders to hang naturally, relaxed, back and down through the elbows (end up with the front of the armpits showing when observing the rider from the side).

c) bent, pointy, relaxed, *heavy* elbows.

d) 'dropable' forearms.

e) vertical hands.

Note These points, combined, make up the core position attitude which allows the energy circuit to be completed (**3.21**). The capital '**D**' front line encourages forwardness in the horse and causes the rider's hands to be in a suitable, passive 'receive-the-energy' mode. If the front line is collapsed, however, and the stomach is pulled back, the body forms a capital '**C**', when looking at the rider from the side; this restricts forwardness in the horse, and the hands take on an undesirable, forced hold-the-head-down attitude.

A few more details

3.19 To elaborate on the above points **a**) and **b**) above. At all times the rider's ears must be kept far from the shoulders and the shoulders far from the ears. It is important to *gently* fill and stretch the nape of the neck – this is emphasized during halts and half-halts. Doing so correctly stretches the spine, giving the lower back (the lumbar region) the necessary tone, and there is less likelihood of it being hollowed. Furthermore, it helps keep the seat bones to point nicely forward into the front of the saddle.

The rider 'On the aids', like the horse

3.20 Filling the nape of the neck is the human equivalent of being 'through the poll' and/or 'on the aids' for the horse. It is an inner energy adjustment. When we are effectively through the poll, it helps the horses step better through the poll, into the bridle and be on the aids. This is inseparable from the concept of pelvic tilt (**9.30b**).

Those precious elbows!

3.21 Right after the seat bones, the elbows are among the most important tools the rider owns. The bent, pointy, heavy elbow is an essential conversion point for the energy. The reins start at the elbows (not at the hand). Collectively, the five points mentioned above (3.18), make for **the optimal attitude to get the elbows connected directly to the middle of our lower back**, which is the elastic anchoring point – the steady base – for a neutral, receiving contact. With suitable heavy-elbow attitudes in conjunction with relaxed, dropable forearms, we can best transfer the horse's forward-reaching energy in the bit directly to the seat bones via the reins and vice versa (completion of the circuit).

3 3.21

Ludwig Koch. Collected walk. Clearly representative of the old standard, 'two-thirds of the horse in front of the rider, one third behind'. Note the presence of the attitudes described in 3.18–3.21

The 'dropable' forearms: drop like a rock!

3.22 Achieving the dropable quality of the forearms causes them to become energy permeable. It helps us become aware of stiffness, tension and energy blockages in the elbow and forearm which is the cause for many contact problems. To get the feeling for achieving this, begin by letting both arms dangle relaxed on each side of the body. Then raise the forearms until the hands come up to the correct height (on the line from the elbow to the horse's mouth when observed from the side). Carry the hands as though the forearms are suspended from thin, weak bungee cords (achieved by having very relaxed, weak-feeling biceps). Then let the forearms **drop down like a rock** from their correct position by making the biceps *instantly* limp and let the arms dangle once again. The elbows should not go forward when the forearms are dropped. However, avoid any fixing of the elbows! The shoulders and triceps do the main job of *elastically* maintaining the steady location of the pointy, heavy elbows when dropping the forearms. Repeat this raising and dropping of the forearms until the feeling is gained for maintaining the relaxed dropable quality even when the hands are carried in the correct position. Another concept that might help, while having the hands in the normal riding position, think of *gently* emulating bobbing a rubber ball in water. Needless to say, none of these ideas are meant to cause the rider to have unquiet hands during riding.

Body energy

3.23 Ride the chest through the shoulders! Ride the hips through the elbows! We could think of keeping the upper body *energy* – and the horse – in front of our whole upper arm and elbows. These are *subtle* physical attitudes, feelings or energy patterns, not external, visible facts.

Receive, but how?

3.24 It is only logical that the elbow should have exactly the same amount of passive, elastic, 'receiving/sustaining acceptance' in direct relation or opposition to the weight the horse puts in the bridle. This allows the hand to remain dynamically in one place (i.e., it is not pulled forward) while affording the horse a steady, neutral, elastic place to reach for and 'come up to'. **This is not a rigid fixing in any way, nor should there be any hint of backwardness in it.** It is a passive, elastic receiving presence (facilitated by the shoulders/triceps) which enables the elbow to receive the forward-reaching energy (weight in the bridle) offered by the horse. Egon von Neindorff would say, 'The hand stands still ... but moves anyway!' – a seemingly typical equestrian contradiction that can only be understood with practical experience.

Ring like a bell

3.25 Stretching the whole position from head to heel, growing taller, thinking of elegance, consolidates our 'withers', seat bones and heels, unifying them into one energy pattern. This is *elastically* emphasized during halts and half-halts. Once we learn to do so correctly, the stretch becomes like a tangible presence whereby our body becomes bell-like, enabling the smallest aids to 'ring' clearly through us and through the whole horse. As a part of stretching, we could think of sitting and kneeling through the heels. This helps our legs to connect to our body energy pattern (**3.15**, **4.29**, **4.82**).

Elegance

3.26 Just to think of the word 'elegance' is like applying a magic potion which draws all our position aspects into one harmonious voice, resulting in a beautiful, practical, unified form. Elegance encompasses elements of both physical and spiritual wholeness – balance, efficiency, ease, nonchalance, self-worth and self-confidence (empty of egotism, arrogance or conceit).

Completing the seat

3.27 **The horse completes the seat** – but we must have that good, steady seat and inner balance *before* the horse is balanced, whereby we raise the horse up to our correctness and balance. When we carry ourselves, horses are better able to carry themselves and us. The alternative lowers us down to the horse's imbalance and crookedness. Ironically, to do so, results in a strange, unwanted 'congruity' in which both horse and rider are comfortable because they are both equally unbalanced/crooked. See photos on page 34.

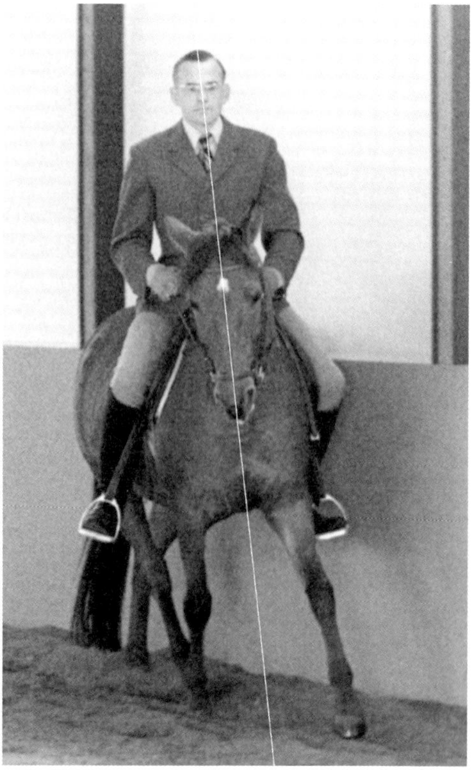

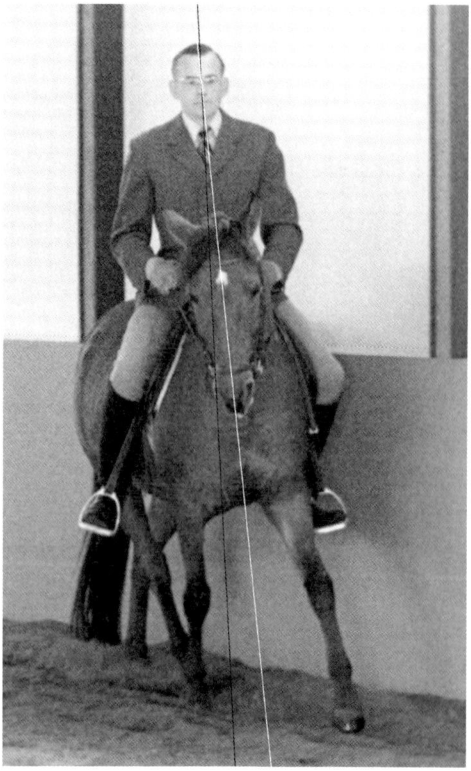

Completing the contact

3.28 The same concept pertains to the contact: **The horse completes the contact.** The foundation of a good, elastic, even, neutral, continuous contact is a viable seat and position which must be present *before* the horse is going well. Then the horse can be helped to reach for and complete that contact. Neither the seat nor the contact can be considered complete unless the rider has learned to help the horse partake in and become a living part of them both.

It's a 'valve'

3.29 Once our body is free of tensions the lower back can begin to act like the essential control valve of the horse's energy. It can determine exactly how much energy is either allowed through, or be more or less restrained (received within) during halts and half-halts. Its effectiveness lies in the upper body's independent telephone-pole like balance, resting evenly on the seat bones. Furthermore, the finesse of this valve-like function only begins to operate properly once independent, synchronized balance has been achieved between horse and rider. The position attitudes for halting while resting on the seat are:

a) Ride the chest through the shoulders/ ride hips through elbows.

b) Have a kneeling attitude.

c) Allow the heels sink.

OPPOSITE PAGE

Top left: *The author on Barty. Shoulder-in right at the trot. The rider is not sitting 'squarely' over the middle of the horse whereby ideal harmony is not present. The horse is leaning in, and the rider is sitting more on the outside half of the horse, see section **3.27**.*

Top right: *The white line runs through the horse's centre.*

Bottom left: *The black line runs through the rider's centre.*

Bottom right: *Here the unsynchronized state becomes clear. To correct this, the rider needs to place more weight on the inside seat bone, and down the inside knee and heel, while rebalancing the horse with a half-halt between the inside leg and the outside rein, then the two lines would merge into one.* Photos, George Ross.

Only once these first three points are correctly implemented, will the final step operate properly to complete the halting procedure.

d) The closing of the hand *briefly*.

3.30

One could think of step **d**) as representing the letter 'T' at the end of the word 'halt' – h - a- l - T! Once the halt is completed, neutralize (relax) the contact and the above-mentioned position attitudes.

Contact woes

3.30 Most contact difficulties can be overcome by assuring a *resting* seat and correcting our upper body, shoulder and dropable-forearm attitudes (**3.18**, **3.22**).

Where to overcome what

3.31 To overcome problems in ourselves, do so in the seat/position. To overcome problems in the horse, do so from back to front with forward energy. These points only operate favourably, however, when we have benevolent attitudes towards the horse.

Outside help

3.32 Tai chi, Yoga, Alexander Technique or Feldenkrais can be useful, complementary adjuncts to riding. They are avenues to help gain control over our bodies; and to help gain an awareness of how our physical and spiritual aspects interact. Riders who have difficulties with balance, coordination or tensions may find these exercise techniques especially useful.

Note See Chapter IX page 141 for further details about influences from the seat and position.

Waldemar Seunig. An exemplary, impulsive passage. The horse is well in front of the rider, the poll is high, the horse's face is in front of the vertical. This 'billboard' is telling it like it is. *See* **6.22**, **6.23**.

CHAPTER IV

Communication: The Aids

Woo Nature with love and selflessness, and all things will be accomplished in their due season.

THE TEACHINGS OF OSIRIS

Introduction

4.0 When compared to most other means of communication, the rider's feeling language of 'aiding' is indeed unique, its messages are relayed mainly through the tactile senses. The following points define the natural and artificial aiding tools, and the various aiding influences.

4.0a **The *natural* tools or instruments** which impart the aiding signals or physical 'words' to the horse are:

- The rider's seat (the body-position and attitudes).
- The rider's hands/arms (aiding via the reins).
- The rider's legs.
- The rider's heart and mind.

4.0b **The *artificial* tools or instruments** are: the **stick** and **spurs**. These are aid 'amplifiers' used to tune or sensitize the horse's responses to the rider's natural tools.

4.0c **The *natural* aids** or signals can be arranged in the following four main categories – weight aids, pressure aids, vocal aids, and mental or psychological aids:

a) **Weight aids:** These are based on the laws of physics to which the horses, *the* master physicists, react instinctively – gravity, dynamic balance, centrifugal force; and the movement of mass to overcome inertia or momentum. These weight signals are imparted via the seat bones and originate from deliberate adjustments of pelvic angle and of body/position and attitudes (**9.29–9.32**).

b) **Pressure aids:** These are made up of leg or rein influences, which rely on a horse's sensitivity to the slightest physical touches or pressures, such as feeling a fly landing on his ever-sensitive body (**4.9**).

c) **Vocal aids:** These are meant to soothe, encourage or, on *rare* occasions, to be stern.

d) **Mental, psychological, abstract or intangible aids:** These aids are based on the creature's acute perception for things metaphysical: those influences which emanate from the rider's mind – made up of thoughts and intentions which are coloured by personality, attitudes, moods or emotions. A horse picks up these fine vibrations either ethereally, or through his ability to sense the slightest changes that thought-power initiates in the rider's body.

Babble or eloquence

4.1 Much as with spoken languages, with aiding we can choose to hobble along with a small, anaemic vocabulary and broken 'Equinish'. Or we can expand our treasury of words and brush up on our spelling and grammar. This enables us to articulate a broader spectrum of concepts, from brilliant colours to the subtlest of hues.

Aids are physical words

4.2 Language, words, or the aids are all similar in this regard: they are merely instruments or tubes through which messages can be conveyed. Physical aiding has little or no value without the rider's clearly-focused mental purpose and benevolent intentions (**4.11**).

Synonyms

4.3 Some synonyms for the word 'aids' are: requests, inspirations, explanations, directives, guides, indications, encouragements, invitations; and as a verb: to help, to assist, to serve.

Antonyms

4.4 Some antonyms for the word 'aids' are: commands, threats, coercions, ultimatums, intimidations, demands, assaults; and as a verb: to accost, to confront, to violate, or to force.

Oh, to be understood

4.5 Among the benefits of basing our aiding on natural law is that, as we become proficient, it is possible to communicate with almost any horse virtually immediately, whether or not they have had any training.

The house of brick: sound attitudes

4.6 As important as they are, technicalities alone will not assure good responses from the horse. But when technique is combined with equestrian tactfulness, a keen sense of timing and having sound attitudes, then ever more harmonious and predictable results begin to occur.

Let's sing

4.7 Aiding is more like singing than speaking, because its effectiveness is highly dependent on the quality of its intonation and sensitivity.

Our attitude affects the tone of voice with which we aid. In other words, it is not so much what we say as *how* we say it.

OK Sparkie; you can do it!

4.8 There is a saying in carpentry, 'Let the hammer drive the nail'. So too in riding, we must let the aids – *small* physical signals – stimulate the horse's *mind* and let him move his own body. Horsemanship is meant to be a fine art. Our main task is to be independent assistants – that is, leaders, administrators and motivators – not common labourers, or physical movers of the horse.

Johann Meixner, Oberberreiter at the Spanish Riding School from 1885–1916. Levade. Indisputably, a Master at work. Notice the closeness of the hocks to the ground, and the softness of the horse's top line.

The power of small

4.9 If a horse-fly weighing a tiny fraction of an ounce can animate a 1,200 pound horse into action, it shows us how illogical it is to think we need physical strength to ride. Clearly, all we need do is to let the horse know that our 'tiny' leg aids are horse-flies, and that the annoying 'flies' will go away when he responds. However, what do we do when he does not respond? Here, a wonderful quote by R. D. Ingersoll shines light on the most basic premise on which horses and, for that matter, we humans learn: 'In nature there are neither rewards nor punishments – there are consequences'. In other words, the totally impersonal, universal laws of cause and effect are always in play.

Logically, the consequence of the horse ignoring the horse-fly (which they seldom do!) is that he gets stung. In the same vein, if the horse does not respond to our normal, light leg aids, the consequence is that the 'spur-fly' or 'stick-fly' will buzz a little louder, or even sting, should that be necessary. It is simply normal for the horse's natural intelligence to respond to those universal cause-and-effect laws; and it is entirely fair for us to use that same principle to help him understand the importance of responding to our leadership. Clearly, we need to use our backup 'flies' tactfully and respectfully – sufficient to help the horse understand that he should respond while remaining mentally calm; yet not so much or carelessly that we frighten or aggravate him into self-protective attitudes (**2.13a** and **b, 4.44**).

Best tool

4.10 Our mind is the most important instrument in the riding task. If something worthwhile is to happen, it is indispensable as it provides that essential '*purpose ingredient*' to our interaction with the horse. **The clarity of the rider's purpose, motivated by will, becomes the horse's reason to act.** The rider's mind, as compelling motivator with its intellectual potency, becomes an extension of the horse's mind and enhances its capacities. The horse's body, with its phenomenal physical power, becomes an extension of the rider's body and similarly magnifies its capacities. This combination fulfils the definition of a true centaur (**4.52**).

Fill 'er up!

4.11 It is essential to develop the art of having gapless concentration or mental presence on the work at hand. That is, we need to produce a conveyor belt of thought fuel, purpose fuel, intention fuel and will fuel. These are indispensable energy sources on which horses run. The moment the rider stops concentrating on a clear purpose – or weakens the willpower to enforce that purpose – the fuel runs out and the horse is *instantly* left abandoned in a vacuum of purposelessness, deprived of the rider's leadership fuel. Easy-going horses will switch off and stop working. Clever horses will quickly take over the leadership role, seldom a pleasure for the rider.

Aimed at what?

4.12 While aiding we must think *only* of our purpose, not of the horse! In other words, we must aim our aids – concentrate our intentions – strictly outward, towards fulfilling our *external* purposes: gait, school figure, exercise (**4.17**). Especially avoid aiming any aiding intentions *directly* at the horse! In other words, think only of what's out there, beyond the horse … and simply *feel* the horse under you – that is, be aware of his response relative to your purpose. The horse will be thankful: 'At last the rider has quit staring at my fingers while I work' (See **6.35**, and the illustration on page 131).

Is it business or personal?

4.13 Our purpose and aiding should be seen as **business** – respectful, clear, tactful, businesslike, impersonal requests: 'Come! Let's go! We need to do this now!'. However, praise may be seen as **personal**, here we may speak directly to the horse, 'Good boy, Sparkie!'. It shows the horse our appreciation for his responsiveness. We need to alternate deftly between the two – either businesslike while aiding, or personal when praising or encouraging. Be a leader, not a pleader.

Think 'exercise' not 'criticize'

4.14 It is more effective to keep the horse's mind on the work by making clear, simple, doable requests, such as: 'Do *this* ... [specific request]', rather than saying useless, purposeless, things like, 'Listen to ***me!***', or, 'Pay attention!' Furthermore, negative requests, those that start with 'no', or 'don't', are difficult for the horse to understand. Positive, impersonal requests usually achieve better results: 'Look *this* way' (into the school, for example), instead of saying, 'Don't look out the door!'; or saying, 'Circle increase' or 'Leg-yield', instead of taking the horse's cutting in as a personal affront, 'Don't cut in against **my** leg!' Take note that, in these examples, the trick is to think of an exercise which **makes sense to you**, and avoid making reproachful commands. Like us humans, horses do not operate very well under the gun of criticism or reproving attitudes. Adopting this approach takes the battle out of the relationship and achieves results relatively effortlessly (see the Note in **4.19**).

Note When using the look-this-way concept when a horse is distracted, besides feeling for the resolution – horse's 'yes' response – another sign that the horse's mind is again beginning to focus on the work is when the ear on the side of the rein aid turns back towards the rider. Another sign the horse is 'zoned in' on the rider's purpose is when the ears become floppy, or when they are, like clock hands, at the ten-minutes-after-ten – the 'Timex' – position.

Power of 'Let's'

4.15 Another helpful concept was contributed by Tom Dorrance. He suggested to use the term 'Let's' before any aiding concept. The difference between, 'Let's do a step or two of circle increase, or leg-yielding' and, 'Get off my inside leg!' is like day and night. By using the term 'Let's', we automatically include our friend, the horse, as a part in our external purpose, and trust in his intelligence and generosity to participate willingly. This gets us away from a dictatorial, commanding attitude, and raises our riding to a more dignified form, that of a true partnership of which we are the leader.

What? and How?

4.16 **What** we ask for defines our leadership. **When** we ask for it, **how** we ask for it, and **how much** we ask for, that must be determined by the horse's nature and his individual needs at any given moment. 'Talent knows what to do. Tact knows when and how to do it.'[1]

Time to choose

4.17 The **what** of our leadership entails that we always clearly choose:

a) The **gait** (the purity, balance, and exact length of stride).

b) The **school figure** (the kind, the exact size, and exact location).

c) The **exercise.** Exercises are a judicious combination of **a**) and **b**), together with transitions, turns on the forehand and haunches. These make up the gymnastic aspects of riding.

Detached and unflappable

4.18 We must avoid being negatively reactionary, and strive towards positive reinforcement instead. It is the rider's calm, detached, unflappable guidance to which horses respond best. It is one of our greatest powers to learn to ignore absolutely *everything* we do not like (never let horses know we notice any of their unwanted responses) while patiently, consistently and repeatedly showing the horse exactly what we do want, and reinforcing suitable responses with immediate praise. This repeated redirecting of the horse's energies should be done without any hint of resentment, annoyance or reproach in our aiding voice. Truly, horses do not stay up all night thinking of ways to defeat the rider. The horse is genuinely trying to figure things out, saying, 'Is *this* what you want? Or is *that* what you want?' etc. When he then does discover what we are trying to explain – and we then praise him – that is how he begins to respond ever more easily, consistently and willingly to our requests.

1 Author unknown.

The bigger distraction

4.19 With intelligence and tactfulness we can convert difficulties into advantages. For instance, when a horse is a world-class tourist, i.e. is readily distracted by things in the environment, all we need do is *distract* him as well, but with the insistent clarity of our purpose, making the aids as clear and rapid-fire as necessary to repeatedly redirect the horse's mind constructively back to the work. In other words, our aids become a greater distraction than the environment. This in no way implies that our aiding should become rough! Furthermore, this approach will not work if we lack consistency or resolve, or if we become annoyed and harden our heart against the horse. It is not productive to use our aids as a weapon of retaliation or punishment, instead of the clear, enabling directives they ought to be.

Note When a horse is being distracted, and we use the 'Look *this* way' concept to correct him (away from the area or object he is staring at), that would be considered a purely **psychological bending aid**. In this case – *as an exception* – it would be absolutely correct to use the rein aid alone (clear, yet *never* harsh!) without any support from the seat/position or legs. For normal bending, however, when a horse is not being distracted, then the usual requirement of engaging the entire 'aiding orchestra' to achieve a bend through the horse's whole body should always be used. This type of aiding would be considered **correct gymnastic bending** (**4.14, 4.84, 5.10, 5.13, 5.16, 5.17, 5.20**).

Corrections? Nyet!

4.20 It is better to think in terms of making 'adjustments' rather than 'corrections'. Adjustments are emotionally neutral requests for change, whereas the concept of making corrections implies judgement – something is 'wrong'. Since horses have no sense of morality they are not wrong; though they might not be doing exactly what we wish.

4.21 Concepts previously placed in 4.21 have been merged in other sections where those concepts have been expanded.

That magic touch

4.22 We must learn to be deft, nimble, quick and timely with our aiding – not hectic.

How much? How often?

4.23 General guidelines for the amount of effort, or the frequency, of aiding are:

a) Aid as little (lightly) as possible – as much (effectively, intensely) as necessary – to achieve the results we want.

b) Aid as few times as possible – as many times as necessary – to achieve (or refresh) the result we want.

The latter point applies only to a reasonable repetition (nudging or pulsing) of a particular aid as needed. It does *not* mean to grind endlessly with one aid or on one exercise (**4.61**).

Be-fitting

4.24 A well-made saddle is fashioned to fit the horse's back and a well-made shoe to fit the hoof – not the other way around! So too the aiding must fit the horse's conformation, temperament and the circumstances like a glove from moment to moment.

'A little dab'll do ya'

4.25 Finding just the right 'amount' and 'tone' while aiding could be compared to the art of mixing colours when creating a painting: a little yellow, a dab of blue – add just a touch more yellow – there, that's just the right shade of green for that leaf! Or, perfect aiding could be seen as a straight line to the goal. In practice, our actual aid might be a little left or right of this ideal imaginary centre line. Beginners tend to make exaggerated corrections, swinging from extreme left to extreme right, and only briefly and accidentally hit 'just right' as the centre line is crossed. The advanced rider also goes from left to right but is better able to adjust the aids quickly and deftly to suit the needs of the moment, and therefore generally hovers closer to the aiding sweet spot.

Gently

4.26 If we think of *breathing* the aids into the horse, it helps us stay relaxed and keeps the lines of *feeling* communication open between the horse and rider. This is especially significant when stronger aids may occasionally be necessary.

Where water flows

4.27 Horses are like water, it is their nature to go where the energy required to do a task is least. Therefore, if they occasionally seem to break out through our aiding 'walls', it is seldom a sign of wilful disobedience. We simply have a weak spot in our river banks; and the horse finds it more comfortable to let his energy leak out there. However, if we tactfully bar every option but our own, causing *our way* to become the path of least resistance, the horses will usually follow it gladly. In this way we achieve our goals fairly effortlessly while avoiding tensions and confrontation. Not to be overlooked, however, is that forwardness in the gaits helps 'waterproof' the river banks.

The mind is amazing

4.28 That which we think of an aid as being, is what the horse will recognize it to be. This shows up clearly in the threefold function of the inside leg: either animating, yielding, or as the passive post around which we bend the horse. These functions can be used individually, or combined to work almost simultaneously. (For bending, changing the bend or changing the rein, see **5.16–5.20**).

Note the 'inside' is the side towards which we wish to bend the horse, irrespective of on which hand we are riding in the arena. Logically, the opposite side becomes the 'outside'.

Making that post

4.29 The inside leg does *not* bend the horse. We bend the horse around it. To make the inside leg become that passive post around which we bend the horse, we must:

- Emphasize the stretch of the body (pillar) above the inside seat bone (the shoulders must remain at the same height while doing this).
- Turn the inside lower leg (toe) in.
- *Gently* snuggle the inside knee a bit more into the saddle flap.
- Allow the 'knee energy' to flow elastically down through the inside heel to the ground.
- Show the inside arm pit a bit more (ride the chest through the shoulders (**3.23**).

Note When may the inside leg be used *actively* during bending?

a) If the horse begins to cut in. In this case briefly think 'circle increase' to overcome this unwanted response.

b) If more forward energy is wanted.

Straight forward

4.30 It is usually not helpful to use both legs *actively* when driving; doing so may even have the effect of inhibiting some horses. However, when driving with the inside leg *actively*, as we should, we must think of sending the horse **straight forward,** *not* sideways towards the outside rein/shoulder. The correct *passive* presence of the outside leg – forming a wall – is central to achieving this straight-forward effect, as it fulfils the need for having equal (or even) value in both legs during driving (**4.47**, **5.30**).

Note The word 'driving' is, of course, quite correct. However, this can easily be misinterpreted as meaning *shoving* the horse forward physically. It is more helpful to think of 'animating' because we want to inspire or excite the horse to move his own body. Furthermore, it is essential to remain physically serene and relaxed during animating. Avoid becoming physically hectic. That tends to obstruct the movement.

Some *'oil plug'!*

4.31 The outside leg plays a small, yet very significant *passive* role. It could be compared to the importance of the oil plug in the oil pan of a car engine. It just sits there passively. It seems not to be doing anything. One simply doesn't even think of it. Yet, without it, there is serious trouble – the engine breaks down for lack of lubrication. It is important to reiterate, however, neither the outside rein nor the outside leg will operate effectively without forwardness in the gaits and without both seat bones being in steady contact with the saddle. This requirement applies to all aiding (**4.34**).

The legs; not *back there*

4.32 It is a common misperception to think that our legs need to be used as far back as possible (near to the horse's flanks or hindquarters) in order for them to be effective. Quite the contrary, the most effective location to apply the driving or animating leg aid is immediately behind the girth. One could even think of pushing the girth forward with the calves while continuing to have deep heels. Avoid pulling the lower leg back and up while driving. It is also generally best to use the stick or spurs immediately behind the leg, not further back on the flank or croup.

A little reminder

4.33 If the horse seems not to notice the passive presence of our outside leg (for example, the croup swings out when bending), we may *very briefly* make it active (a quick 'tap-tap' with the stick, or 'prick-prick' with the spur on the outside) just to re-affirm the outside leg's presence, after which it must *immediately* return to being passive again. See sections **4.27**, **4.76**, **4.77** about escaping of the horse's outside shoulder.

Only forwardness brings understanding

4.34 The outside rein and leg can only do their job properly as a containing river bank in the presence of sufficient forward energy.

The truth of this becomes particularly clear when riding young horses. Here, neither strong outside aids alone, nor leg-yielding from the inside leg (thinking to bring the horse better to the outside aids) will bring the desired results. Furthermore, overbending the neck to the inside really makes things worse. Counter-bending could work but it is a relatively poor temporary fix. It is forwardness, therefore, that most often readily resolves the situation of horses escaping through the outside aids.

Behind the 'eight ball'

4.35 If we are visionary – thinking, preparing and acting well ahead of time – we seem to have all the time in the world. If we tend to be reactionary, however, and wait for trouble before we act, our aiding usually comes just that bit too late, leaving us constantly scurrying about playing catch-up. We end up riding from error to error, instead of from improvement to improvement, and relinquish our leadership because of this. As an antidote, it is essential to maintain clarity of purpose and ask the horse for many small, *meaningful* requests to which we expect responses (**4.56**).

Not aimless ...

4.36 Experimenting with the above concept is like frequently testing the water. Is the horse responding to each little request? Doing so keeps the lines of communication alive and helps the horse's mind stay on the work.

OPPOSITE PAGE

Above: *Richard Wätjen, working canter on the snaffle.*

Below: *Richard Wätjen, collected canter on the double bridle. Regarding these two photos, Wätjen pointed out that one of the technical differences between the working canter and collected canter can be readily discerned by the distance between the diagonal pair of legs, the second phase of the canter sequence (in this case the left hind and the right front).*

Something about socks

4.37 We certainly can have a forward-urging influence from the seat/position. It is an encouraging, '*passive-positive*', 'going-with' or participating attitude. However, we can no more push the horse forward with an ***active*** seat than we can pick ourselves up by our own socks. The seat's influence, though very real, should be absolutely passive and quiet relative to the horse's back and, other than its good effects on the horse, it should be invisible to the observer (**9.17**, **9.18**).

Seat bones; they only transfer

4.38 The seat bones are only implements which transfer energy – they themselves do not create energy. The rider's core – the lower back and the front line – can encourage forwardness *passively*. If they seem not to have sufficient influence, then active legs aids come into play and, if necessary, tune the horse with stick or spurs. For details see **4.44**, **9.24**, **9.33**.

Less work

4.39 Ninety per cent of ensuring adequate forward energy involves:

a) The rider's joyful, positive mental attitude (**4.11**, **4.53**);

b) Staying out of the horse's way physically by being harmonious with the horse's movement with the seat/position;

c) Having gentle, neutral, allowing hands.

Under those circumstances, only ten per cent of forward energy needs to be supplied by the *active* leg aids (always with engaged seat and position). Clearly, if **a**), **b**) and **c**) are **not** present, then, unhappily, ninety per cent of the rider's effort must be produced by the seat and legs.

It's automatic ...

4.40 It is, of course, common knowledge that the hindquarters supply the forward energy in the horse. Nevertheless, in nature horses do not say to themselves, 'OK, hindquarters, engage **now!** so I can get away from this hungry lion!' Horses simply respond to their immediate circumstances – briefly summarized in: 'I'm out of here!' Thus, when riding, it really doesn't help to think of aiding the hindquarters or hind legs. The hindquarters have no brain! Instead, just send the whole horse forward by aiding the horse's mind. We do so by exciting his spirit via signals to his body. Let the horse worry about where the energy comes from! His nature will know what to do. We just need to say, 'Let's go **there**, Sparkie!', and the hindquarters will engage automatically, and the horse's forward energy, balance and alignment will spontaneously come under the saddle.

Responding *because of understanding*

4.41 **Good energy** comes about through patient, correct training and a steady, consistent routine whereby the horse comes to *understand* what is wanted. Therefore the horse remains *calm* and he is able to **respond** willingly to the rider's reasonable requests. Calmness means the horse is content with the rider's presence and with the task he is asked to do. With good riding, horses become willing participators instead of subdued slaves who constantly need to be shoved and cajoled into action. Because the horse's own natural talents are cultivated and engaged, over time the work can become truly gymnastic, resulting in beautiful, powerful, elastic movement (see Chapter VIII, Inspiration for Animation).

Reacting *because of coercion*

4.42 **Poor energy** emerges when the horse is forced. This is especially so when horses are crammed together with contradictory aiding – being blocked in front while being driven up from behind. The rider is mainly interested in the horse's outline and head position which results in an artificial erection of the head and neck. On the one hand, this approach may result in the horse appearing perfectly obedient and 'pretty', but he has become a soulless automaton. Dull and lifeless, he does his job to avoid the wrath of man. On the other side of the coin, he loses trust in his leader, and goes into self-protection mode. The first premise of horsemanship – *calmness* – is not present. The horse does not understand. Therefore instead of responding, he **reacts** out of duress, in a stressed, kneejerk manner. True gymnastics can not be manifest because the work has underlying tension which shows up in hovering gaits and tight backs, upon which the rider's seat can not help but bounce. To the untrained eye, the movement of an over-revved, tense horse may seem spectacular. To the horseman, however, it is untenable.

Belly to belly?

4.43 It takes time and experience to cultivate one's eye and be able to differentiate between right and wrong.

a) **Right** Riders who *quickly* and *clearly* assert their leadership with a few emphatic aids, backed up by the stick or spur when necessary. This pertains especially to achieving response to the forward aids.

b) **Wrong** Riders who lose self-control and senselessly vent their frustration on the horse;

– or who torment horses with indecision, inconsistency, meaningless and endless pushing, shoving, whacking, spurring, coarse half-halting;

– or who tyrannize the horses with constant 'sawing' on their mouth – forcefully 'trapping' them between the bit and the driving aids (riding with the foot on the gas pedal and the brake at the same time) – thinking to get the horse 'round' and his head down 'in place';

– or who coerce horses to take on attitudes which are mentally or physically injurious to them, such as riding deliberately with the face behind the vertical (the 'Rollkur').

These are truly the greatest unkindness and unfairness against the horse. Honourable riding is not made of such!

Note To the untutored eye, the above two examples of right (truth) and wrong (falsity) may appear to lie side by side. Yet, for the connoisseur it is like trying to compare ordinary glass with diamonds, or ormolu-plated trinkets with solid gold. They are, simply put, irreconcilable opposites. We live in a world where it is not unusual for good to be vilified as being evil – and where falsehood and deception are proclaimed and celebrated as being good.

'Tuning': acceptable versus unacceptable – the details

4.44 a) Without forward energy there is no horsemanship. Accordingly, 'tuning' or sensitizing horses to respond to our animating influences is an indispensable skill each rider needs to develop. Horses can be tuned or dulled very quickly. In either case the result has little to do with the horse, but rests solely on the talent and level expertise of the rider. Lack of skill or carelessness regarding this subject quickly causes matters to deteriorate. When poorly handled, horses quickly lose confidence in the rider which opens up a whole can of unwanted worms. Clearly, one size does not fit all! To be successful, all aiding must be deftly matched to the horse's temperament and to the circumstances at any given moment.

b) Every animating aid could be seen as a small tuning or **re**tuning of the horse. The most essential part of successful tuning is clarity of purpose and consistency. These are indispensable components of fairness and kindness.

c) When dealing with lethargic horses or those who have been seriously dulled, it requires yet greater finesse and experience on the rider's part. Because the timing of the aid and the clear black and white, carrot-and-stick contrast between the moment of tuning and the praise *immediately* afterward is ever more critical to success. **Contrast is the strength and clarity of the aid!** With the vast majority of horses, especially more sensitive ones, an occasional little tap-tap reminder with the stick or quick prick-prick with the spur is sufficient to achieve better responsiveness. However, when *initially* changing the listless habits of lethargic or seriously dulled horses, the tuning may briefly need to be somewhat more substantial. In this case, it is best to use only a single, more emphatic stroke with the stick.

An effective exercise to help awaken brighter forward responsiveness is the halt/trot-on transition. With tact and finesse we need to encourage the horse to trot on directly from the halt without any interim walk steps. We must take care, however, not to ambush or surprise the horse as that would only cause fright and tension.

d) What parameters define acceptable tuning? Though the *initial* tuning of very lethargic or seriously dulled horses may briefly need to be more substantial, **tuning has nothing to do with aggression or punishment.** The use of the stick or spur are only there to explain to the horse the importance of responding to small aids (**4.9**). The hallmark of good tuning lies in its **absolute brevity, clarity** and **consistency**. It is important to know that horses have an uncanny sensitivity for fairness and for reading the actual intention of our heart. They will not be deceived. They do not know about social graces – only about truth and unvarnished honesty. Thus, genuine benevolence of the rider's heart, combined with calm emotional detachment is central to success. There must be absolutely no malice, anger, reproach, vengeance or frustration involved. Our aiding needs to be applied with unconditional good will and unaffected, honourable purpose in our horsemanship. With these attitudes as backdrop and with the seat well engaged (**9.26**), we must give a clear, *active* animating aid with the leg alone as our encouraging inner-aiding voice says, 'Let's go! More forward **now**!' If the horse does not respond, we must *instantly* re-aid with the leg and *simultaneously* give a reminder with the stick – making it absolutely clear we *expect a response* (**4.23**). When the horse does subsequently respond, however slightly, silence the leg *immediately:* ***stop – giving – the – aid,*** and praise sincerely. Praise, that is, showing *genuine* appreciation and gratitude, is an indispensable partner to successful tuning (**2.1**, **7.22**). This entire aiding cycle should take less than a second. It may be repeated as necessary to *incrementally* raise the response to the desired overall level. It will be found helpful to want to feel (expect) a clear forward *surge* from the horse to each and every animating aid. After each tuning, the next forward request should be given *lightly* with the leg alone (seat/position always correctly engaged at those moments). This gives us the chance to evaluate whether the horse is beginning to respond without needing backup reminders from the artificial aids. Should the response be lethargic, then the whole tuning procedure needs to be repeated until good responses are achieved from just normal, light leg aids alone. Our appreciation can be underscored by making some walk 'on-the-buckle' breaks after gaining some better responses from this tuning procedure.

e) How can we know whether our tuning approach has been acceptable? Here we should consult the expert: the horse himself! When the above-mentioned guidelines have been implemented with a sincere, benevolent heart, the horse will remain mentally calm while increasing in forward responsiveness literally within only a very few minutes on smaller leg/seat/position aids alone. The stick or spur soon become less needed. In this way, under the deft leadership of a competent rider, the horse's willing contributions are tactfully evoked and his childlike enthusiasm to please begins to blossom. From then on, normal tuning (a little tap-tap reminder with the stick) should be all that is needed to assure adequate levels of forward energy (see '**b**' above).

f) Our tuning becomes unworthy and unacceptable, however, when selfish ambition drives our actions, or when we approach the horse as an adversary to be vanquished. Then the aid is given with underlying anger, reproach or resentment. Or, even when the aids are given out of emotional exasperation (having to 'get mad' before asserting ourselves), they will similarly not achieve satisfactory results (**2.6**). The horse feels accosted and will likely react in a negative, self-protective manner. If a horse seems to need frequent, strong tuning with stick or spur during any one ride (or worse yet, every ride), it is a sign the work is of the poorest order. Either the rider's attitude is unsuitable, or the necessary consistency, skill and sensitivity is lacking whereby the horse is repeatedly more dulled than tuned. The horse then either ignores the strong, nagging aids and becomes ever more anaesthetized to preserve his sanity; or, if continually pushed unfairly, his rightful disapproval will surface.

g) As a final note, when sending the horse forward – especially during tuning – it is crucial to have a clear giving attitude with the hands. To be concerned about keeping the horse's head down in position during tuning – or to think of half-halting or balancing before consistently good responses are achieved from the driving aid – only confuses the horse and sabotages the simple clarity of our forward-tuning message. Next, it is important to reiterate that the natural leg aid (always with a well-engaged seat/position!) should be given with a quick, clear, yet *light* pressure (**4.9**). This applies even if the horse has been seriously dulled. Because, if we use strong leg aids during tuning, the horse will always wait for that stronger aid before beginning to respond ('Uh-oh, I better get going', says the horse, 'The rider *really* means it now!'). Therefore the desired progression of responding to *ever smaller, invisible aids* will not occur. See **4.59**, **9.8**, **10.43**, **11.22**; and Chapter VIII, *Inspiration for Animation*.

Delegate!

4.45 When we always rely on a calculator or an electronic navigation system, our brain quickly becomes lazy and incapable. The horses will similarly become mentally lazy and incapable of contributing unless we persistently *delegate* to them their task in the partnership and refuse to do the thinking for them. Thus, by delegating we help the horse become a thinking, contributing partner in the work. To delegate, we need to be clear about the allocation of duties. It is the rider's task to bring the horse clearly up to an energy level of, let's say, 8 (on a scale of 1 to 10) and then to show the horse that it is *his* responsibility to continue to move himself at that level. It is indeed *not* the rider's responsibility to constantly 'keep the horse going'! The rider's job is to show the horse what is wanted and then to delegate that. Delegating is done by leaving the horse strictly alone after he responds. That is, we must neutralize, silence or relax the leg aids and – equally important – trust the horse implicitly to continue to do that delegated task on his own. Only once the energy level drops below 7 should we again remind the horse of his part of the bargain by refreshing the energy level back up to 8. At first, the horse may lose energy quite quickly, after just one or two steps. But with consistency and quiet persistence the number of steps between reminders soon increases, as the horse begins to recognize he is left alone as long as he maintains his energy level between 8 and 7 on his own. And because horses love to be left alone by the rider, they will begin to seek out that quiet place on their own, where we continue to encourage them with the gentle 'shadow aid' and praise them for their contribution (**4.53**, **9.25**). However, if we are untrusting, or lack clarity, consistency, or resolve, or are asleep at the switch half the time, we will not succeed. Or, if we think we have to push, push, push all the time, we seal our own fate. The horse will simply switch off and say, 'Fine. Push me, if you can!' The skilful rider knows how to say, 'You move yourself. I just want to sit here!' The principle of delegating applies to all aiding concepts. It gives horses the space to figure things out for themselves, the confidence to act, and nurtures their desire to contribute willingly (**4.8**, **4.60**).

Ludwig Koch. Canter pirouette left.

How often?

4.46 Irrespective of how often we need to re-correct or re-adjust the horse, after each aid, we must give forward with *both* hands *absolutely equally* (2mm, 1/10") and trust the horse that he will continue with the request on his own (see **5.17**). Only through clarity, persistence and consistency is ground progressively gained (**6.5**).

A motto

4.47 A handy motto for delegating and maintaining the energy level is: 'Up to eight, and delegate!' Monitor and refresh! No nagging! No holding! No pushing! No shoving!

About fairness

4.48 Once the horse has responded to either the stick or spur, we must avoid giving that *extra* aid 'just for good measure'. It is unfair. It not only tends to extinguish the horse's willingness, but it can justifiably raise the horse's ire.

Are you open?

4.49 It is essential to drive only when horses are in an open, accepting state of mind (**2.16**). This applies especially to very sensitive or nervous horses. If they are not yet receptive, we must *rest* in our seat ... and *wait* ... passively ... patiently ... and only then, when they begin to accept our presence in the saddle again, and are calm, driveable, not tense or rushing, should we judiciously re-introduce the driving aids: drive a bit, get a response, coast a bit. (Important, see **6.32**, **6.33**, driving sensitive horses). This resting and waiting, however, applies only to the driving influence. It does not mean to relinquish our overall leadership purpose. We must always continue to choose the gait, school figure and exercise. When horses rush, it is important not to reject or withdraw ourselves physically or mentally from that quick movement. Instead, without judgmental attitudes, go with the horse harmoniously and then, from that synchronized (though fast) state, ease the horse back to a more suitable rhythm/tempo.

That acceptance zone; indispensable

4.50 The same applies to training in general. We must work horses only within their mental *acceptance zone* – where they can understand and partake. Outside that zone we fail to achieve good results because the horses are no longer in a state to be able to contribute willingly. Give the horse time to think.

Just 'so'...

4.51 When the aiding is either too brief, too small, lacks clarity, determination, or purpose, it has little or no useful effect. When the aiding is too long, too strong, or too aggressively applied, a disconnection between horse and rider occurs and the aids do not go *through* the middle of the horse's being. Such aids are mentally rejected by the horse at a deep level and go around the outside of them, so to speak (**4.41**, **4.42**). Egon von Neindorff would warn, 'Bring the horse up to the highest limit, but don't push him over it'.

Finer degrees

4.52 We should strive to refine our aiding to the point where – if we look at aids as a range of numbers – the smallest fractions are sufficient to have the horse respond, and not always aid with coarse increments of whole numbers. When we have it right, the distinction between our aiding request and the horse's response seem to merge into one and the same act – the horse seems to be connected directly to our mind: the centaur (**4.10**).

I'm with you ...

4.53 A **shadow aid** is a small, passive, maintaining influence, an encouraging presence which helps the horse to know that he was good to respond to our last request, and that he should continue to do that on his own. For example: the active aid says, 'Come on, let's go more forward!' Then, as the horse responds, the shadow aid softly whispers, 'That's right, continue-on just like that.' The shadow aid is technically made up of the 'maintaining seat' (9.25). But more importantly, it is exemplified by the rider's steady, mental presence, continually monitoring the performance relative to a clear purpose. Consequently, the horse is not left in a vacuum of leaderlessness in the moments between our active aiding. Horses are astoundingly – almost magically – aware of a rider's mental presence in the work (4.10, 4.11).

4.54 Concepts previously placed in 4.54 have been merged in other sections where those concepts have been expanded.

Incarceration or freedom

4.55 Holding is restriction – incarceration. Freedom is space – love! When we have this right, the horse senses, 'I'm allowed to be myself, but I welcome and love my rider's benevolent guidance'.

Preventing

4.56 'Preventing' is just another form of holding. Instead, we always need to allow the horse to make his mistakes honestly (just for a split second, or for a stride or two) and *only then* re-aid him to show him again exactly what we do want. Repeat this cycle again and again, until the horse starts to make (or maintain) the right choice on his own. On the other hand, it is helpful to make timely preventive adjustments *before* they are needed. For example, we can refresh the horse's balance and carriage or perpetuate the canter before it is lost; or we can deliberately make small changes of bend, position alterations, or transitions. Such rejuvenation can be as frequent as necessary to help the performance become smooth and steady, while avoiding any hint of holding or preventing. This is central to keeping horse and rider independent, yet in living attunement with one another over extended periods.

Sincerity

4.57 Because of their candid reflection, horses help us to see the actual state of our 'inner horse'. But to benefit from this, we need to be open and absolutely honest with ourselves and with our intentions towards the horse – no hidden agendas. When we are true to ourselves and live in accordance with our conscience, we become true to the horse – and the horses, then, invariably are true to us.

Oh, to be free …

4.58 It is best to steer clear of emotional attachment to success or failure of any aid, or to our work in general. We must dare to lose what we have gained, and patiently set about re-finding it repeatedly. **Only by daring to release (or neutralize) after each aid** – implicitly trusting the horse's intelligence, generosity and willingness – will we ultimately have what we want without either fearfully or ambitiously having to hang onto it. This is the key to delegating and achieving willing participation. It invites the horse to become a thinking contributor to the work and to assimilate and integrate the rider's adjustments mentally and physically into the innermost parts of his being. Adjust them, and trust them! We are indeed liberated when free of all attachment (**11.21**).

The very life-breath of aiding

4.59 This concept can not be sufficiently repeated, understood, or practised. It is the very life-breath of effective aiding and successful horsemanship: **with a clear purpose in mind,** Give an aid – get a response – stop giving the aid. But remember the shadow aid (**4.53**).

An elaboration

4.60 To elaborate on the above guideline: *give an aid*. Here we could say: 'give an aiding concept'; because frequently **a small series of aids** needs to be given with the whole aiding orchestra to complete a certain desired effect. Then, 'get a response': be sure to achieve a *resolution* to each and every aid. This means we need to aid in such a way that we help the horse to respond by saying, 'Yes, OK, I can do that' – only then is the aid truly *resolved* within the horse. Finally, 'Stop giving the aid': honestly neutralize, silence or relax the aiding tools (hand, seat, or leg), and trust the horse *unconditionally*. Ninety-nine per cent trust is no trust at all. Even if one initially should need to repeat the aid again just one or two strides later (and that repeatedly!) trust the horse each time again by neutralizing the aiding system between every aid.

Note This principle is identical to the very basis of sound health and development of any living organism. The DNA tells a cell to start growing, and then to stop when it has reproduced. If there is no 'start' to reproduction and replacement of old cells, the organism dies. If there is no 'stop', cancer develops. One could deduce, that mindless, ceaseless, nagging aids are a form of equestrian cancer.

Nix that holding

4.61 Monitor and adjust, or 'refresh' the horse as needed – hold nothing! Live by the quantum theory of aid giving. Act now! Expect and get a response from every aid. This is exclusively the rider's responsibility. Avoid looong, drawwwn-ooout, yaaawning, haaaanging, presssssing aids. If, at times, it takes a bit longer to resolve a particular aiding concept, impart little nudges or pulses of aiding energy to the horse to avoid getting stuck in the mire of hanging-on to unresolved aids, while being persistent, consistent and insistent about achieving the desired result. In this way we avoid congesting the aiding pipeline so that the next aid is unencumbered by previously unresolved aiding requests. (Important: see **4.49**, **4.83**, **6.32**, **6.33**, **8.7** about aiding sensitive horses.)

Little air bubbles

4.62 It is helpful to think of making little 'air bubbles' in the rein aids – little neutralizings, or little gives, little relaxings, little starts-and-stops within the asking – so the horse never feels there is anything to hang on or be against. Such aiding is subtle and should be invisible to the observer.

What comes first?

4.63 It is essential always to get some result from our natural aids *first*, and only then use the 'hearing aids' (stick, spur), if necessary. In other words, we must bring our will and desire (purpose, intention) clearly into action through our body first, *before* we tune the horse with the artificial aids. We must *live* our intention unambiguously with every cell of our body! Say what you mean. Mean what you say.

That worked, so …

4.64 If you like what you got; keep doing what you did.

Elephant ears?

4.65 We should strive to speak as softly as possible, while listening as loudly as possible. We do this by having huge 'elephant ears' on every aid we give, straining to hear the slightest responses from the horse *while aiding*. This allows us to sense that critical moment when to stop giving the aid as the horse responds. If we are not feeling and listening for the horse's response *while* aiding, horses lose their desire to contribute. We are best able to listen or feel when we remain mentally calm and physically relaxed: *serenity* (3.1 through 3.5).

Shades of light and dark

4.66 It is good to aspire to classical ideals but that does not mean to be ineffective. On the other hand, being assertive and effective is good but that does not mean to be aggressive or crude.

To lead = to listen

4.67 Only when we ourselves are guidable – that is, open to the needs of those we are leading – are we able to be appropriate, effective leaders.

Both sides; always!

4.68 We must *constantly* channel or sandwich the horse laterally between the neutral, *passive* two-sided presence of our inside and outside riding tools. With both seat bones, legs (knees!) and reins we gently hug or surround the horse like a 'potato in a sock'. This constitutes the river banks through which we direct the horse's energy. It is the central, *passive* foundation from which all aiding is given. Both sides – both sides – both sides – always both sides!

Marbles, anyone?

4.69 The undesirable opposite to the potato in a sock happens when, for lack of forwardness in the horse, or the rider's inability to establish a smooth, continuous contact with their seat bones, legs and reins, the horse becomes like a marble in a tin can. He then rattles around loosely and uncontrollably between the rider's aiding tools, bouncing from wall to wall, so to speak.

Choosing in's and out's

4.70 The **diagonal aiding concept** is the foundation for the entire aiding system. Accordingly, even if we are riding on a straight line, and *deliberately* do *not* wish to have a bend in the horse, it is nevertheless essential *always* to choose which is the inside and outside. We do so by having a *little* emphasis on our own diagonal aiding influence. Just being aware of the **inside seat bone** (51:50) and leg, and being aware of having the **outside rein**, is sufficient to cause the diagonal principle to work.

Diagonal influence

4.71 The diagonal concept 'inside leg *and* outside rein' comprises four major influences:

a) It can be used to balance.

b) It can be used for aligning or straightening.

c) It can be used deliberately to set up the two-track positions.

d) It makes the guiding aids efficient and operable.

Diagonal aiding does not necessarily mean that we must change the bend, nor change our leg position. Its power lies in the invisible, *subtle* interactive, counter-balancing, inter-communicating pressures or influences between the diagonal aiding tools which bring about the desired changes in **a**) through **d**). The inside leg must 'know' the outside rein. The outside rein must 'know' the inside leg. Any adjustments to the horse especially regarding **b**), and **c**), only make sense when they are made relative to riding absolutely clear, accurate school figures (**4.74**, **5.31**).

One-sided influence

4.72 **Unilateral aids:** seat bone, leg and rein on the same side. Used *passively* these aids stem sideways-drifting from the intended school figure (**4.68** always applies anyway!). This concept can be experienced by riding full-school on the second (inside) track, or by riding on any straight line away from the school walls (**5.37**). Unilateral aiding can also be used deliberately for leg-yielding. In this case the leg becomes the *active* initiator of the lateral requests. The rein is usually only passively confirmed, just *thinking* of the rein is usually enough. After all, it is called leg-yielding, not rein-pulling. **It is essential that this *confirming* of the inside rein *does not alter* the bend in the neck.** The rein influence is very subtle!

Oxymoron

4.73 For normal riding both seat bones should be even (50:50). When emphasizing one seat bone a bit more (51:50), we must *not* lighten the other one. In other words, the *emphasizing* is the important part, while avoiding the lightening! Riding is replete with such apparently counter-intuitive, seemingly illogical things which can only be clarified and experienced through practice.

What is the difference between straightening and halting or half-halting?

4.74 If halting, half-halting and straightening (re-aligning crookedness) entail the use of diagonal aiding, what is the difference between them?

- **Straightening** (re-aligning crookedness) What does the seat do when straightening? To whichever side the croup evades, the *opposite* seat bone should be increased with a bit more *forward* emphasis to realign the horse, 55:50. What do the legs and reins do? As the seat influences are applied, *increase* the pressure of the leg (on the side of the evading croup) while simultaneously increasing the *presence* of its diagonal partner the rein (on the side of the evading shoulder).
- **Halting or half-halting** There must be *equal* pressure in both legs (relative to each other) and *equal* pressure in both reins (relative to each other). If necessary, the inside leg (animating) *or* the outside rein (half-halting) may be used actively (by nudging, or pulsing), but the pressure must remain even. Remember, either active leg *or* active rein, not *both* active simultaneously.

Note The terms 'equal value' or 'equal influence' can be substituted for 'equal pressure' (**5.29**, **5.30**, **5.31**).

Move forward or move over

4.75 What is the most basic difference between leg-yielding and driving? For driving: both legs must have *equal* pressure (or value). For leg-yielding: the leg from which we want the horse to yield must have *greater* pressure than the other. However, we should always *gently* hug the horse between both legs during leg-yielding – the leg from which we want the horse to yield asks, the other leg, though lighter, gently receives (4.68). (For suitable leg positioning see **5.19** to **5.22**).

Either 'and', or 'to'?

4.76 For guidance, increasing energy (balance, half-halt), and straightness we need to think inside seat bone/leg **and** outside rein. For turns on the forehand, circle increase, leg-yielding, or shoulder-in we need to think inside seat bone/leg **to** outside rein. It is essential, however, to be aware of receiving that forward/lateral energy (generated from the inside seat bone/leg) with the outside rein (seat bone/leg!). Be sure to **have that outside rein** during such exercises to avoid losing alignment of the outside shoulder and therefore the balance. Do not allow the neck to bend more! See *Figure 4.1* below.

Which arrives first?

4.77 (*Figure 4.1*) **Incorrect work** The shoulder is leading (escaping) during leg-yielding from the quarter line to the wall of the arena. The shoulder will arrive at the wall first. This problem is usually associated with dominant use of the inside rein which causes overbending of the neck in front of the withers. The inside seat bone/leg and outside rein are not interacting correctly.

(*Figure 4.2*) **Incorrect work** The croup is leading (escaping) during leg yielding. It will arrive at the wall first. Here the inside leg and outside rein are too dominant.

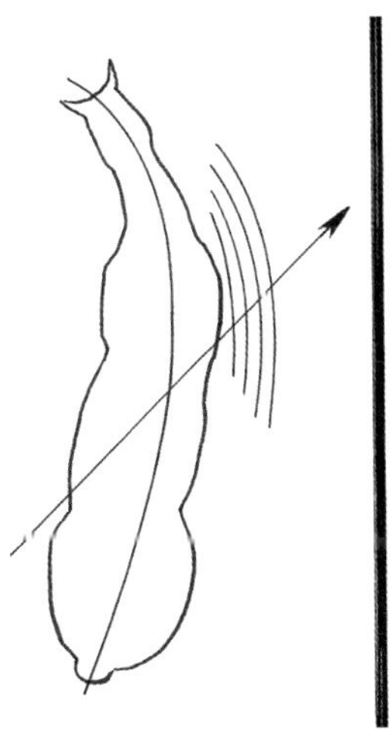

Figure 4.1

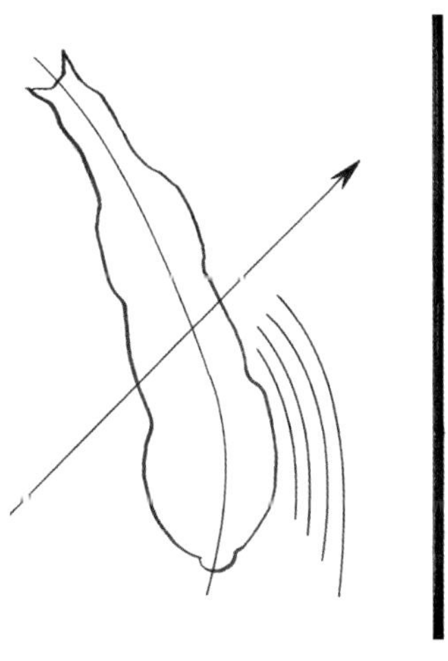

Figure 4.2

(*Figure 4.3*) **Correct work** Here the ribcage leads the way. The shoulder and croup will arrive at the wall at the same time. There is a good balance or inter-relationship between the inside and outside aids.

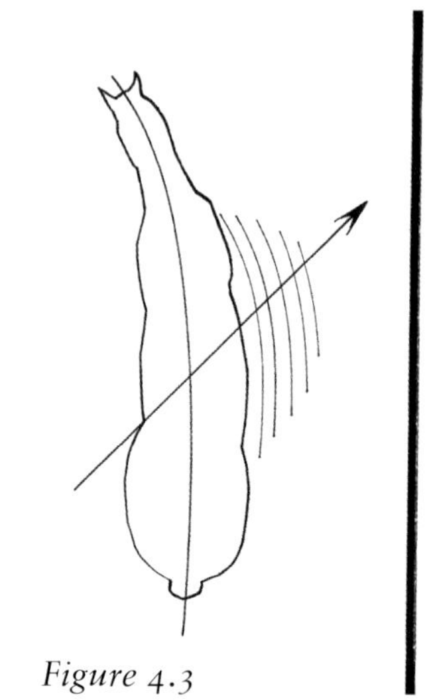

Figure 4.3

Note For both circle increase and leg-yielding, think of having the horse's outside ribcage leading the way to arrive at the wall (or to the larger circle) first. However, as long as it is not escaping, it is acceptable for the outside shoulder (the horse's forehand) to lead the way just *slightly*.

Most misused or most neglected?

4.78 **The most misused aid is the inside rein.** First, it is commonly misused as a dominant steering aid by pulling the horse in the direction one wishes to go (instead of using the whole aiding orchestra, and letting the horse flow through the 'waterproof', bent channel of the river banks (**4.27**). Second, it is incorrectly used as the dominant aid during leg-yielding, to do the job the inside seat bone/leg and outside rein should be doing. Third, the inside rein is misused to do shoulder-in, by shoving it against the neck/withers/shoulders on the inside (instead of using inside seat bone/leg and outside rein, while keeping the inside rein slightly away from the neck (**4.76**, **4.77**). Such misuses of the inside rein block forwardness of the inside hind leg and result in 'broken' gaits.

The most neglected aid is the outside leg. Because the inside leg is so often over-emphasized in the rider's mind due to its important role as animator, the outside leg is simply forgotten about. It is interesting to note, however, that the outside leg only very seldom actually needs to be used either strongly or actively. Technically, the outside leg's ineffectiveness may be traced to a weak outside seat bone, it being either lighter, or that it lags behind (**4.30**, **4.31** and **4.68**).

It's the law ...

4.79 Natural Law is in charge, not us humans! Every action has an equal and opposite reaction. So too in riding, **cause and effect** rule. Force elicits counter-force. We can not be refined enough that the horse will not match and exceed our level of sensitivity. We can not be rough enough that the horse will not match and exceed our roughness, blow for blow, and be quicker and stronger than we are. If we want to overcome the horse's tension or apparent 'againstness', it works wonders to emulate water: softness overcomes hardness. 'A soft answer turns away wrath, but a harsh word stirs up anger'.[2] The wise rider knows how to avoid confrontation by skilfully absorbing, dissolving, or diffusing the horse's resistant energy and redirecting it usefully (**4.27**, **5.9**, **5.31**, **6.12**, **6.14**, **6.28**, **7.7**, **7.8**). The following point provides an example.

Overcoming 'against-ness'

4.80 If the horse is tense and against the hand, we should avoid trying to keep his head down with a stark, hard, downward-boring, or backward-working hand. It is fine to *allow* the hands to be low under such circumstances, but they should be absolutely neutral in that low position (**3.18**, **3.21**, **3.22**). In the presence of an open

2 Proverbs. 15:1

front line, the hand (elbow) needs to assume a steady place, yet not be stark or blocking (**3.31**), as the driving aids encourage the horse to reach better into that contact. Also, rather than trying to get the nose 'down' or 'in', *think* of helping the horse reach (stretch) with his mane from the withers up and forward towards the poll, by encouraging forward energy from good working gaits. If the horse should speed up, the half-halt will regain the balance/rhythm, after which we must 'give while driving' again (**7.6d**). Repeat as necessary. The horse will soon settle in and begin to reach independently and elastically for the bridle once again.

4.81 Concepts previously placed in 4.81 have been merged in other sections where those concepts have been expanded.

Knees 'on'!

4.82 The rider's knees should be in *gentle, relaxed* contact with the saddle at all times. It is essential to avoid making this into a cramped gripping of the knee on the saddle flap. The correct quality allows the body/seat energy to flow down past the knee, through the heel to the ground. This is best achieved by resting relaxed on the seat bones; by opening the hip joints wide outward; and by turning *only* the lower legs inward (without involving the thighs!) until the feet are about parallel to the horse's sides (feel this, do not force it). This allows the knees to be on the saddle flaps without the inner thighs pinching and restricting the movement of the horse's major back muscles. When the knees are correctly on the saddle flap during driving, the animating energy from the lower legs is more readily converted into balance and carrying under the saddle. When the knees are off the saddle flap, however, the animating energy is more likely to cause the horse to become unbalanced and land more heavily on the forehand.

Bright, crisp … creamy-smooth

4.83 Use bright, crisp, pulsing 'hot potato' aids for dull horses. Use creamy, smooth, caressing leg aids – like 'emptying a tube of toothpaste' out the front – for nervous or sensitive horses.

The hands: job description

4.84 What may the hands do?

a) Half-halt deliberately (**3.29**, **6.30**, **6.31**).

b) Assist deliberately with the bend or straightening.

c) Guide passively.

All else is unwanted fiddling which usually has just one agenda: to achieve the *symptom* of getting or keeping the horse's head down without regard for correct engagement of the whole horse. This 'get-the-head-down-at-all-costs' obsession is one of the great offenses against the horse's nature. It does not belong to worthy horsemanship.

Note After each of the above three points, we need to repeat the refrain, 'While *always* addressing the whole horse with our aiding orchestra and underscoring forwardness as necessary!' For exceptions see **4.19**.

End of the line!

4.85 The rein aids must be at the *end* of the aiding system, not the beginning. They are largely meant to receive and direct the energy which is already either naturally offered by the horse or generated by our animating aids. In other words, all rein aids must be well based in (they must be overcome by) adequate forward energy in the horse. This can only be achieved in the presence of predominant, well-suited seat/position/leg attitudes. This, however does *not* mean we need continuous strong or *active* driving; nor should we have the horse running off his feet.

Gracefully, please ...

4.86 Rein aids should be given gracefully and *elegantly* – somewhat like the *quality* with which a ballerina expresses herself with her arms.

Disabled, at last!

4.87 Isn't it amazing how horses usually go instantly better when the hands are incapacitated because the rider has put both reins into one hand (**5.28**, **5.30**, **5.31**).

Doing 'nothing' well

4.88 We could see the hand as nothing more than an innocent bystander, a witness to the state of the horse, as opposed to being a central figure. Only those who have learned to truly appreciate this through years of earnest practice, know how devilishly difficult it is for the hand to play its refined, *passive* role – doing its 'nothing' well! The old adage 'less is more' certainly applies.

Three sides of the coin: the extremes

4.89a **For timid or diffident riders** Horses need and respect leadership. The most essential aspect of being the leader of the partnership is to have clarity of purpose, and to be decisive in carrying out our objective, even if we do not feel entirely sure or competent. We must make up our mind, put *our* program (our purpose or intention) into the computer, and go for it! It is crucial to get responses from our aids *right now*, today, regardless of how inexperienced we might be. Because only when we get some kind of response (large enough that we notice it!) *from each and every request*, will we then, through practice, gradually improve and refine the way in which we achieve those responses. When we are hesitant, indecisive, or irresolute, the horses either ignore us or quickly take over the decision-making role. They then put their program in the computer, which is seldom a pleasant or useful experience.

4.89b **For well-meaning but overly-conscientious or overly-cautious riders** On any given day we must simply do our best. We are always good enough for the task of learning just as we presently are. If it were not so, no one would ever begin to learn anything for fear of making mistakes or harming the horse. As long as we act in good faith and have a kind heart towards horses, they readily absorb the rider's many struggles and not-so-perfect aiding on the way to better understanding and skilfulness (**2.2**). It is useful to remember that experts may be pretty good, but no one is perfect. 'Never let what you can't do interfere with what you can.' Albert Einstein.

4.89c **For strong, confident riders** If we could but realize the strength that lies in *benevolent*, fair leadership, which gives space to those we are leading and allows them to be themselves, a whole new, wonderful world of perspective, feeling, and experience opens up to us. When serenity rules our hearts, it enables us to listen to the horse's needs and gives us the composure and confidence to let the water of time develop the seedlings of the creature's willing contributions. In this way the horse's small, honest gifts – which we acknowledge with sincere praise – can grow naturally into the beautiful plants and blossoms of an elegant performance. We can no more succeed in forcing a horse to produce beautiful, elastic, balanced work, than we can force an oak sapling to become a glorious, tall shade-tree in a few short years. We can only diminish ourselves and regrettably damage the horse when we are impatient and disrespectful, and give in to our negative emotions, or to our greedy, self-serving ambitions. Our task is called leadership, not dictatorship. The horse is our conscience.

Tête du Cheval blanc. *Théodore Géricault (1791–1824). Musée de Louvre, Paris.*

The author on Barty. Shortened working trot, right. Nicely bent while going deeply through the corner. Here the horse is more 'upright', and is laterally more 'even' under the rider's seat than in the photos on page 34. But the poll has gotten too low. More energy is needed to bring the horse better in front of the rider, and therefore gain the desired raising of the poll. Photo, George Ross.

CHAPTER V

On Bending and Guiding

Introduction

5.0 The concepts of bending and guiding are perhaps intellectually quite clear, but in practice they are often muddled. This causes much difficulty for both horse and rider. Though this subject clearly belongs under the heading of 'aiding', this chapter has been dedicated solely to bending and guiding, specifically to describe the difference between these two concepts. Some useful exercises are also suggested to help clarify this distinction in practice.

Definitions

5.1 – **Bending** refers only to forming a lateral 'arc' or 'bend' we intend to achieve in the horse's body or spine from head to tail (left bend or right bend). This concept also involves lateral 'flexion' (bending or softening) behind the horse's inside ear and jaw.

– **Guiding, steering, and turning** are all synonyms for another concept: the task of navigating the horse in the direction, the school figure or path we intend him to follow.

Can they bend? Have a look!

5.2 Are horses able to bend in their bodies, their spines? Though there seems to be some controversy about this topic, it is fairly easy to ascertain. However, we need to avoid the blinding effects of preconceived notions. For example, we just need to take the time to quietly observe horses when they are lying down, curled up in their stall; or if we have the opportunity to see horses scratching themselves on their flanks or 'where the foal sucks'; not to mention seeing large horses turn themselves around in a cramped wash-stall or, more amazingly yet, in a horse trailer! That we as riders may have difficulty accessing such lateral spinal flexibility is a different matter altogether. But, just like achieving correct deep bending or flexing of the three major joints of the hind legs, essential for lowering the croup and achieving true collection, bending horses laterally in their spine should not be forced but needs to be tactfully invited and encouraged (10.4, 10.25–10.38, 10.42).

What comes first?

5.3 First, forward energy, assure balance, *then* the guiding/bending aids become easier and achieve better results.

A truck?

5.4 If the horse steers like a truck, we have not helped him to go sufficiently forward in balance.

Vital!

5.5 The motto for all **a**) guiding aids, **b**) halting, **c**) half-halting, or **d**) rein-back is: Both reins even (equal *value*, even *influence*), keep the neck the same. This means we must avoid any unintentional altering of the lateral bend in the neck during the above mentioned actions. **Always keep the neck *laterally* the same!** Unintentional changing of the neck causes loss of alignment and balance, and poor directional control of the horse (5.28, 5.29, 5.34, 5.35, 10.10–10.12).

Optimum

5.6 The time-honoured criteria for the ideal amount of bend in the horse's neck is that we should see no more than a *glimpse* of the inside eye and nostril rim. For exceptions during training, i.e. temporary corrective measures, see **6.3**.

Like a babe in a cradle

5.7 Always cradle the horse's shoulders well between the seat bones, knees/legs and reins during bending or changing the rein. The foundation of successful cradling is to be resting evenly on both seat bones. Be especially aware of the *new* inside leg and the *new* outside rein before and during bending or changing the rein.

No 'pop-out'

5.8 To avoid loss of balance when bending, always maintain the alignment of the horse's outside shoulder within the stream of energy. It is a common mistake to allow the outside shoulder to pop out. However, take care not to block forwardness with the outside rein while tending to alignment, or when re-aligning the outside shoulder. Besides the primary goal of bending the horse around the inside leg at the ribs, the aim is to bend the neck halfway up between the withers and poll – making it laterally hollow where the inside rein crosses the neck. We must avoid lateral overbending just in front of the withers/shoulders (**4.76**, *Figure 4.1* on page 71). Though alignment (straightness) and balance are inseparable partners, alignment comes first. See **4.28**, **4.68**; and Chapter X: Stages I (**10.10**), II (**10.18**), III (**10.23**)

More bending?

5.9 When asking for more bend, do so gently. It is not necessary to make the aid stronger, harder or harsher. After all, we are only looking for a greater *degree* of bend. Think of bending only as a request or invitation. If the horse seems against the inside rein, do not force the bend. Repeatedly interrupt the asking with small, tactful gives, little 'softenings' or 'diffusions', even before the horse has given! It is a clear yet subtle, living request, entirely void of confrontation (**4.62**, **4.79**). The inside rein asks, the outside rein allows and/or limits the amount of bend as the moment requires. Be sure to have all the concepts stated in **5.10** well organized. 'Feathering' can also be used (**7.7**, **7.8**). Review the details about causes for unevenness in the reins and crookedness and how to overcome them (**7.11**, **10.11**).

Bending needs a foundation

5.10 Though it is entirely acceptable to use an active inside rein as part of the bending influence, it is by no means always necessary to do so. Before using an active bending aid with the inside rein, attend to the following points:

a) First emphasize the inside seat bone a bit more (**51:50**) by stretching the inside 'pillar' (**3.12**) and by showing the front of the inside arm pit a bit more (chest through the shoulders);

b) Turn the inside toe inward and snuggle the knee *gently* into the saddle flap (**4.82**);

c) Stretch down through the inside knee and heel; have a little more weight in the inside stirrup iron (let the inside heel *say* the same thing as the inside seat bone, **a**);

d) 'Flow'[1] the inside seat bone energy towards the horse's outside shoulder.

Though mentioned separately, these points come into play simultaneously, orchestrally. They help us experience the importance of basing all aids in appropriate seat/position attitudes, rather than aiding mainly with the extremities: arms/hands/legs. See **Note** to **4.19** for exceptions. Once the bend has been achieved, we must neutralize or equalize the above aids (in that bent state), and send the horse forward through the 'bent channel' formed by our seat bones/legs/reins. Only if the horse loses the bend or

1 Use of the word 'flow' in this regard was contributed by Sue Terrall.

if we deliberately wish to change the bend should we reapply the above-mentioned bending influences.

Nuts and bolts

5.11 A well-let-down, resting seat together with suitable position attitudes are indispensable for effective guidance. This mainly involves being able to direct the energy from either seat bone independently, or both seat bones simultaneously. As an integral part of this, we must be able to turn the upper body from the waist in the direction we are going; and/or be able to have a more forward emphasis from one hip/seat bone *with* or *without* turning the upper body – that is, 'turning the bar stool'. See Wilhelm Müseler's *Riding Logic*: exercises lying flat on one's back on the floor, lifting one hip off the ground at a time.

A little shift

5.12 A horse will only consistently follow slight shifts of the rider's weight when the horse is balanced and when the rider remains absolutely central during the guiding influence (no leaning, tilting, collapsing anywhere) (**7.8**).

Seat guidance

5.13 The technicalities for guiding or turning the horse from the seat are:

a) Rest equally on both seat bones, then emphasize the inside hip more forward ('hips parallel to the horse's hips').

b) Turn the upper body in the direction you intend to go (shoulders parallel to horse's shoulders). But do not exaggerate this, and be sure to keep the outside shoulder nicely back and down, as opposed to rounding it forward while turning the upper body *slightly* in.

c) Without changing the location of the seat bones, increase the stretched presence of the inside leg through the heel in the stirrup iron (do not jam it down, just *feel* it gently);

d) While sending the horse nicely forward, we must *point* him in the desired direction with our hips (seat bones) and navel energy. *Feel* and point the *whole horse* to go **there** i.e. ride the horse's body, not just the head and neck! The entire aiding orchestra is involved in this – literally every cell in the rider's body! Yet, this has nothing to do with strength or being busy. Guiding is a *subtle* influence, forcefulness will not bring success (**6.8**, **7.8**).

e) Doing some turns on the haunches can be helpful to get the feeling for the orchestral aiding influence needed during general guiding.

Note Just as with the rein aids, when aiding from the seat, do not ask more with the seat than the horse easily and *willingly* follows; doing more than this causes a disconnection to occur between horse and rider (**7.8**).

'Ride' there, or 'lead' there

5.14 We should think of *driving* the horse in the direction we wish him to go. Do not **pull** him there with a predominant inside rein. Should it be necessary, the inside rein may, nevertheless, subtly **lead** the horse where we wish him to go. This applies especially to young, green horses. Here the inside rein is opened away from the neck with an **inward-forward** (*not* **backward**) attitude, like opening a kitchen cupboard; while the outside rein *gently* keeps the neck laterally stable (prevents overbending). Both reins must have equal *value* while leading to avoid accidentally changing the bend in the neck during guiding! At first, this may appear to be a contradiction. But, no indeed, there is a vast difference between inward leading, and one-sided backward pulling, or unwanted, accidental changing of the neck bend while guiding.

To master this is bliss!

5.15 Two of the most important guiding concepts to be mastered.

a) Turning the horse inward. Think: 'Tiny circle, *here*!'; or 'Change the rein through the circle'; or 'Turn on the haunches'.

b) Move the horse away from the inside leg. Think: 'Circle increase'; or 'Leg-yield'.

By thinking of these simple, doable exercises, regardless of where you are in the school, guidance becomes easier and confrontation is avoided (**4.14**).

Serpentines and changing the bend

5.16 *Figure 5.1*, overleaf, illustrates the concept of how to change the bend and the rein while riding a large serpentine through the whole arena, from long side to long side. It shows the importance of 'cutting back' *before* crossing the centre line (making a 'ribbon candy' form). The capitalized letters pertain to the diagram.

a) Begin the change of bend about 1.5m (4–5 feet) before the centre line. This is initiated with an effective half-halt just before beginning the change of bend at A.

b) Between A and B, we may 'bend in' with the inside rein *if necessary*, while simultaneously 'squashing' the horse's ribcage out with the inside seat bone/leg (**5.10b, c, d**). One could think of this influence as being a brief circle increase without actually doing it. Be keenly aware of receiving the horse well on the *new* outside rein; and having the outside leg nicely back (**5.20b!**).

Once the horse has bent in – that is, softened to the bend without cutting in against the *new* inside leg.

c) Stop the bending influence (relax the **bend-in, squash-out** idea).

d) Between B and C, push both reins forward equally (2mm, 1⁄10") while sending the horse well forward through the 'bent channel of the river banks' in the new direction of the intended school figure (see **5.17**).

Important Points **a**) and **b**) above should be applied *strictly* separately. An effective half-halt **a**) must be completed *before* the details in **b**) are implemented. Using **a**) and **b**) simultaneously only causes confrontation and tension. All the concepts described

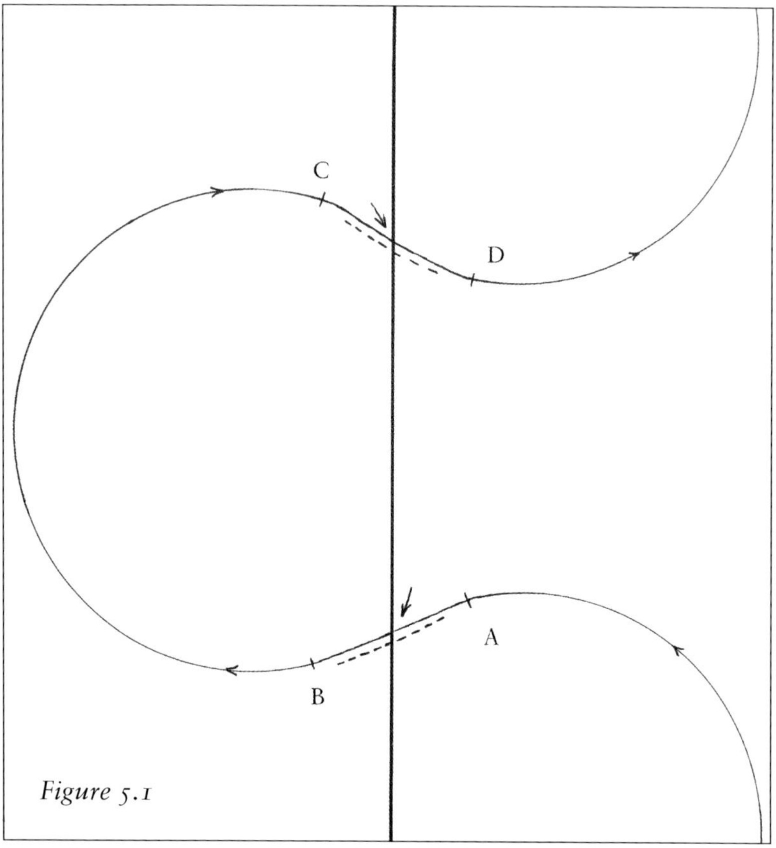

Figure 5.1 This diagram shows key points for changing the bend and the rein for a 'ribbon candy' serpentine from long side to long side. About four such loops would fit in a standard 20x40m arena. It will be found helpful to practice this exercise at the walk first. For details see 5.16, 5.17.

above can also be used *in a more subtle way* any time we want to change the bend or the rein.

Give on both reins equally

5.17 Avoid the common mistake of giving more on the outside rein after the half-halt, or giving more on the inside rein after the bending aid. Both reins should be given forward *absolutely evenly* towards the horse's mouth after *any* and *every* rein aid; encouraging and fully trusting the horse to follow his nose through that bent channel. Be sure to make long, honest, confident, *trusting* gives with the reins of at least two-seconds duration (count 'twenty-one, twenty-two'). Avoid making quick, abrupt, 'shotgun' gives.

Is the bend resolved?

5.18 If the bend is resolved, the horse will neither cut in nor drift out when both reins are given forward equally; rather, he will follow his nose in the direction of the bend.

Heel energy

5.19 When bending the horse: we should direct the inside heel energy towards the horse's inside front hoof (that is, the heel energy only, avoid pushing the whole lower leg forward; also do not jam the heel forward or downward!) The outside heel energy should be stretched elastically toward the horse's outside hind hoof. This is especially helpful during canter work. However, here too, do not jam the heel back and down.

Leg position

5.20 a) **For work on straight lines, when *no* bend is wanted in the horse,** both the rider's legs should be in the same position – directly opposite each other and directly behind the girth. This is also the best location for animating the horse. This even placement of inside and outside legs describes an ideal. When horses are crooked or one-sided, one of the legs may *initially* need to be placed back a bit to help achieve linear, or **mechanical**, straightness and/or maintain alignment (10.10, 10.13, 10.14).

Important review 4.70, 4.71, regarding always choosing which is the inside!

b) **For any work when a bend *is* wanted in the horse,** the rider's inside leg should remain forward at the girth, and the outside leg taken back by about a hand's breadth. This is a general, time-honoured guideline which applies across the board, irrespective of whether single- or two-track work is being asked for (see definition of single- and two-track work, 10.8).

Note The actual amount of position differentiation between the inside leg's forward placement near the girth, and outside leg's backward placement depends on the sensitivity of the horse and the level of training.

Ah, yes – the exceptions

5.21 There are some exceptions to leg positioning, however. When introducing leg-yielding or turns on the forehand *during the very earliest stages, literally for just the first few training sessions* for either horse or rider, it may be helpful to put the yielding leg (the one we want the horse to move away from) back a little *temporarily*, until the lateral yielding concept is better understood. But, as soon as possible, good lateral responses should be obtained with the rider's yielding leg in its normal, forward, inside-leg position at the girth. Furthermore, other than for the briefest of corrective measures, once the horse is sufficiently advanced to do shoulder-in, the rider's inside leg must always remain forward at the girth, with the horse beautifully bent around it at the ribcage. See *Figure 10.8* on page 172.

Not exactly right

5.22 If the rider feels the need to put the inside leg back in order to get a (supposed) shoulder-in, it is a sign that the horse has not been brought correctly up to the outside aids *in forwardness* from the inside seat bone/leg in single-track work, and that we have not bent the horse properly in his body. Such a pseudo shoulder-in could therefore be considered nothing more than a very rudimentary, even poor, form of leg-yielding. This is often seen in conjunction with the common error of overbending the neck to the inside. See **4.76**, *Figure* 4.1 on page 71. A fine exercise to discover the practical logic of the above concept, is to alternate between riding single-track voltes, then 6–10 steps of shoulder-in, then another volte, etc., back and forth between the two concepts up the long wall of the school. When this exercise is done correctly, the inside leg should not need to be moved from its correct, forward, at-the-girth location. See **Note** for **10.31** about doing this same exercise in the Stage III attitude, which is particularly useful to help overcome a horse's leaning-in on circles. Review sections **10.33–10.38**. See *Figure 10.8* on page 172.

Another task for the outside leg

5.23 While bending the horse around the *passive* post of the inside leg (placed at the girth), the standard guideline to 'put the outside leg back by a hand's breadth' not only *passively* guards the hindquarters from swinging out, but it also gives the horse's outside ribcage the necessary space to expand (bulge) outward during bending. Furthermore, though the inside seat bone should have more forward emphasis during bending, it is essential that the outside seat bone *energy* always remains well forward over the knee on its own side. Its energy must not lag behind (**3.14**, **3.15**).

Stop that bulge!

5.24 With the above concepts in mind, if we do *not* want the ribcage to bulge or expand to the outside (such as occurs when riding in the direction of the horse's easy-to-bend, hollow side [i.e. the side of the empty rein]), then the leg (remember the seat bone!) on that bulging side needs to be placed *temporarily* a little more forward near the girth (even though it is the outside leg), while *thinking* of bending the horse around that leg (just *hint* at that, feel it, do not actually do it). This helps the horse's straightness and therefore allows the energy to arrive more evenly into both reins. As the horse begins to reach habitually more evenly, our legs can then be placed normally once again – inside leg at the girth, outside leg further back, as needed (**5.20b**). See photo on page 162.

A little less bend, please

5.25 Any time we wish to *lessen* the amount of bend in the horse (for example, from being *over*bent to the left), then we should think of bending the horse in the opposite direction – that is, to the right (which *immediately* and *temporarily* becomes the inside)

– until the desired degree of *diminished* left bend is achieved. The same concept would apply if we wish to deliberately straighten the horse from having a normal left bend, to end up being straight (no bend at all) while yet remaining on the left hand in the school. Here again, the right side would *temporarily* become the inside, until the desired degree of straightness (no bend at all) has been achieved. In such cases the changes (as to which is the inside) need to be made quickly and deftly.

What to do when …

5.26 If the horse is 'empty' or hollow on his left side, then, when riding on the left hand with a left bend, if the horse escapes out of the right shoulder, it is a sign balance and alignment have been lost. To correct this, we must animate the horse with our *left* leg – 'tap-tap' behind the left leg with the stick, if necessary. Remember to think **straight forward** while animating (**4.30**) and being very aware of having the right rein (seat bone/leg). The right rein may be kept passively, or if necessary it may give an active half-halt. An alternative concept is to think of doing a little leg-yielding from the left leg while having the right rein (seat bone/leg). The reversed correction would hold true, when the horse's 'empty', or hollow, side is on the right.

A contradiction?

5.27 If the recommendation in **5.26** seems contradictory, it is important to remember, the horse can only understand and respond well to the *outside* aids when balance, based on forward energy, is present (**4.34**).

Watch those guiding pitfalls

5.28 The most common errors in guidance are:

a) Dominating with one rein – usually the inside one.

b) The inability of the rider to remain evenly let down on both seat bones *at all times*.

c) Lagging behind with the seat bone energy on one or both sides.

d) The upper body is *not* turned in the direction the rider wishes to go (**5.13b**).

These tendencies are more likely to happen when stronger aids are being used.

The 'one-chunk' horse

5.29 Since false, one-sided *rein* aids are responsible for many common guidance problems, it can not be sufficiently recommended that we learn to **make both reins absolutely** *even* **in their** *influence* (i.e., equal in *value*, as opposed to necessarily being even in weight or pressure), especially during any guiding (3.8). When striving to keep the horse's neck and shoulders laterally stable during half-halting or guiding, we need to keep both hands directly opposite each other, right there above the withers, each remaining strictly on its own side of the neck. Then think of guiding the whole horse inward, **like one chunk** (head, neck, shoulder, body, hindquarters *one piece*) with emphasis on turning the horse's shoulders/withers *not* his head. This must be done without taking the outside rein across the centre of the neck to the inside. Let the quality (or energy pattern) of the outside rein be aimed directly at your navel as you guide. This idea should in no way cause the horse to turn his head to the outside, nor should it bottle the horse up. This simultaneously helps maintain the alignment of the horse's outside shoulder within the stream of energy. Keep the withers right there between the seat bones/knees/legs; and the base of the neck steady and straight between the reins (hands). If a horse does not respond readily to the turning influence from the *outside* rein aimed at the navel, a judicious tap of the stick behind the *inside* leg (energy!) while briefly reconfirming the outside rein (this re-establishes balance and alignment) will help turn the horse (5.13). It may help to *think* 'turn on the haunches'. Indispensable to the success of these concepts is to assure that the horse is always reaching steadily into both reins because of adequate forwardness. There is no aiding concept in which being **brief and effective** is more important than during guiding; riders often get stuck and end up giving long, pulling, hanging aids on the horse's mouth (7.9, 10.35).

Test it: equal influence (value)

5.30 How can we know when we have achieved equal influence (value), especially when the weight in the reins may at times be uneven due to temporary, unresolved one-sidedness in the horse? Clearly this can only be tested and understood while we are riding with a clear purpose in mind. When we are in the process of riding transitions, for example, if we are able to assure:

a) That the horse's neck remains the same (i.e. the lateral bend does *not* change).

b) That the horse remains exactly on the chosen school figure.

c) That the horse remains straight (no lateral crookedness or evasions of the croup or shoulders), then we have caused even influence (value).

During any of the above-mentioned effects, it is essential that the aiding remains absolutely independent. This evenness must end up being an integrated, resolved state within the horse! For solutions on how to help the horse become even in the reins and under the seat, see **7.11**.

Synchronizing the hands

5.31 To better understand what having '**evenness in the rein influence while guiding**' means, experiment with the following:

- bridging the reins;
- touching the knuckles together;
- placing the hands on the neck (withers);
- having the inside of the forearms *gently* against our hips;
- holding a riding stick across our thumbs;
- riding temporarily with both reins in one hand;

- having both reins in one hand while laying the free hand on top of the one which holds the reins.

We need to use these concepts until the *feeling* for having this essential, steady, even two-sided rein guidance is better developed; and its benefit on the horse is experienced. Through working with these ideas we discover how the circuit between the two reins becomes complete, literally like a loop – a constant intercommunicative, interactive counter-balancing, one with the other. Through this it will be found that the seat and leg influences will also be more readily understood by the horse. We need to experiment with these good effects and learn to transfer them to the work when the hands/reins are separated once again. These concepts also teach us how to guide with harmonious seat/leg and unified rein influences, without using the ruinous effects of one-sided rein aids for any guiding, steering or turning. The importance of having two-sided rein contact at all times could be compared to an electrical circuit. If the contact is lost on one side, the circuit is broken and, guess what? No lights – nothing works!

Easier? Why?

5.32 The reasons why the horse goes better with the reins unified (5.31) is: first, because it minimizes the lethal effects of inappropriate one-sided rein action; and second, because the circuit is shorted at the hands (the horse's energy comes up one rein to one hand, flows directly across to the other hand, and goes down that other rein, and back around again). This takes the arms and the entire upper body largely out of the equation. The moment we separate the hands, however, the energy circuit between the reins must now be able to travel unrestrictedly through the arms, shoulders, and the rider's body as well. This opens a whole can of worms of having to deal with correct posture and suitable attitudes with our arms, shoulders and entire upper body. Tensions, stiffness, or one-sidedness, *anywhere* in the rider, impedes this energy circuit from functioning freely as it should. This is the root of many problems (5.13).

There are two *circuits*

5.33 There are actually two energy circuits or loops we need to contend with:

a) The above-described circuit looping between the reins.

b) The circuit of forward energy which travels through the horse's spine, arrives at the bit, travels up the reins to the elbows, goes through the rider's spine, and ends up connecting to the horse's back once again via the rider's seat bones (**3.18, 3.22**).

Bend only deliberately!

5.34 It is a common error to end up changing the neck laterally (bending it more), when all we actually wanted is to guide (turn, steer) the horse. The only time in which the neck should be changed laterally is:

a) during *deliberate* bending or flexing;

b) during *deliberate* straightening; or

c) during *deliberate* changing of the bend from one side to the other.

Note The neck is, nevertheless, a less important part of bending. We need to bend the horse especially in the body without losing the essential unity in the spine from the tail to the poll (5.37–5.39).

Bending; guiding: strictly separate

5.35 We must be able to change the school figure without changing the bend. We must be able to change the bend without changing the school figure. The bending aids may not turn (steer, guide) the horse. The turning (steering, guiding) aids may not bend the horse. They are mutually exclusive. We need to keep their individual function organized clearly, neatly, and separately, in our minds. Guiding and bending certainly may be *deliberately*, harmoniously combined, but they must not be muddled up.

It's logical!

5.36 Of course it is acceptable to have a bend to the inside, but just because the horse is bent does not mean we have to turn in that direction. How else could we ride shoulder-in, or ride on a straight line with a bent horse? Furthermore, just because a horse is *not* bent in the direction we want to go, does not mean we can not turn if we should wish to. How else could we ride a horse on any school figure in counter-bend?

Exercises for discovering the difference between bending and guiding

5.37 To discover the difference between the bending aids and the guiding aids, several exercises are described in these next three sections: **5.37–5.39**. It is best to practise these on horses who are at first level or above. The three exercises described below are to be done in **single-track**. None of this is two-track work (see definitions in **10.8**). Initially this work should be done at the walk on straight lines going 'full school', on the 'second track'. **Full school** means to ride on the 'first track' right next to the wall, around the entire perimeter of the riding arena. Full school, **second (or inside) track** means to ride parallel to the arena walls, but about 1.5m to the inside, away from the walls, doing so around the entire perimeter of the riding arena). To benefit, it is essential to ride school figures accurately! Do these exercises until things begin to go relatively smoothly; probably three or four times around the school.

The first exercise is done like this:

a) First: Ride all the way around the school on the left hand with a plank-straight horse. Second: Ride *one* 10m circle at B or at E in the middle of the long side. Do not bend the horse anywhere, not even in the corners of the school nor on the 10m circles.

b) Next, while remaining on the same hand in the school (left), using the same school figure, do the same exercise as **a**), but now do it with a *counter-bend* (bend the horse to the outside, to the *right*) all the way around the school, even in the corners and on the 10m circles. Be sure to keep the horse tracking straight (single-track work), the hind legs must follow exactly in the same path as the front legs.

c) Next, while remaining on the same hand in the school, using the same school figure, do the same exercise as **a**), but now with a *correct* bend in the horse (bend to the inside, *left*) all the way around the school, even in the corners and on the 10m circles.

d) Next, change the rein across the diagonal of the school. Now do the same exercises – **a**), **b**), **c**) – while going around the school on the *right* hand; in mirror image. Start with the plank-straight horse, then go to the counter-bend (that is, bent out, *left*) and finally end up with true right bend. Here again, do each phase until things go smoothly.

Important Do this exercise just once a week, or so. Do not over-practise it because, especially when these concepts are new to the rider, horses readily lose forwardness, their backs can get locked-up, and the gaits suffer. Most work should be done in forwardness in single-track work, in all three gaits.

Another version

5.38 Another variation on the above exercise to help discover the difference between the bending aids and the guiding aids, is to guide the horse at the walk on a straight line (full school, second track, for example) while repeatedly changing the bend. Do so *slowly and deliberately*, however, and take at least five or six steps to make any change. For example, take six steps to go from being straight to having a bend; then staying in that bend for about five or six strides before changing back to straightness; then stay in straightness for five or six strides, before bending to the other side. Be sure to stay exactly on the chosen school figure, or the exercise is not useful. Especially, strictly avoid any rapid left-right bending – sawing – of the neck.

A more challenging version

5.39 Finally, the last and most challenging exercise to help understand the difference between bending and guiding is:

a) Walk on a 10m circle with a counter-bend (place circle on the centre line, keeping the figure equi-distant from all the arena walls);

b) Walk on the same circle with no bend (plank-straight horse);

c) Walk on the same circle with the correct bend to the inside.

Do each phase for several circles to get the feel for it, and do this on both hands until it is better understood how to guide the horse without changing the bend in the neck/body. Here again, be sure to have the horse tracking straight during this exercise – both the hind legs and the front legs must be aligned on the circle line! It is a common error to allow the croup to go to the inside of the circle line during counter-bending. This is to be avoided because it causes serious loss of forwardness!

Summarizing the orchestra

5.40 In summarizing this chapter on bending, we must be sure to have correct seat/position attitudes, and understand that guiding involves the whole aiding orchestra. The **main guiding aids** are the **inside seat bone/leg** and the **outside rein** – well based in the outside seat bone/leg; and keep **the outside shoulder** nicely back and down (this does not mean to turn the upper body outward). Just *thinking* of the outside rein is usually enough, because during guiding the reins should act identically, with one purpose, like Siamese twins joined at the hip (5.30). Tuck the horse nicely into the outside aids with that inside leg (*think* 'circle increase', while passively limiting that very request with the outside aids). These are especially important points when riding horses on their more difficult-to-bend, less-preferred, or stiff, side. When applied in conjunction with feathering on the inside rein, most horses will readily become soft and even (7.7, 7.8)

Egon von Neindorff, extended trot rising – a wonderful moment exemplifying how the horse, when correctly ridden, demonstrates beautiful, uphill, balanced freedom under rider.

CHAPTER VI

Training Concepts

Nature can not resist our quiet, patient, consistent discipline.

AUTHOR UNKNOWN

Introduction

6.0 Horses show us by their demeanour whether our interaction with them makes them feel balanced and content, or awkward, unsettled and frightened. But even after twenty years of perfect training they still never know *why* things feel better – or worse. This is because their way of thinking is largely reactionary, rather than more visionary, conceptual, or deductive such as ours can be. As remarkable as horses appear to be at solving certain problems, when they feel ungainly under saddle, it would never occur to them to deduce, 'Oh, I know what's wrong. I feel a bit unbalanced. So if I generate more forward energy, I'll regain my balance and feel better again!' Instead, the creatures live very much in the present moment. They are highly impressionable and are inclined to react either to the stimuli of internal biological needs or to external events happening in their immediate environment. Under natural circumstances, for example, horses might go energetically and nicely balanced – showing-off their spectacular stuff – only briefly when excited by a clap of thunder, or when wolves threaten the herd, or out of sheer joy in life which may spark the herd to gallop and buck playfully on a crisp, autumn morning.

6

6.1

Other than such instances the horses tend to just plop along lazily on the forehand, with minimal effort, over to the next clump of grass for a little lunch. It is Nature's perfect efficiency, to use energy only when absolutely necessary. In light of this, the significance of the rider's motivating leadership to give purpose to the work and to help ignite the horse's forward urge can not be overstated; it is the very life-blood of horsemanship. Each rider needs to develop the talent of exciting the horse into being energetic at a time when the horse, by nature, sees absolutely no reason for engaging his energies. That is one of the most indispensable ingredients in the art of riding: skilful animating. To reiterate: **the rider's clarity of purpose, motivated by will, gives the horse reason to act.** See chapter VIII and **4.44a–g** for details on how to animate the horse.

An avenue of approach

6.1 If it is good for the horse, it is always good for the rider. The converse is not necessarily true.

Trust

6.2 Trust in the horse's intelligence; generosity and ability bring rich rewards. Unbelief and distrust beget precisely what they anticipate: noncompliance, and untrustworthiness.

Exaggerations

6.3 Training the horse operates on a principle of *momentary* exaggeration. One could see exaggeration as being a form of explanation. Once the explanation has been understood, the exaggeration is no longer needed. It is somewhat like overbending a coat-hanger wire, just a little, so that when it is released it remains bent just the right amount on its own. For example, on the hand where the horse is easy to bend, bend him less. On the hand where the horse is difficult to bend, bend a bit more (regarding this aspect, be sure to see **5.9**, **5.13**, **6.8** and **7.8**). A horse who is prone to rushing would be worked deliberately more slowly; a horse who is lazy would be ridden more briskly, etc. Needless to say, such exaggerations or tuning of the horse should be used judiciously and be uncompromisingly brief. They are to be seen as no more than '*Temporary Corrective Measures*' (TCM's)! We need to get to normal riding, aiding and responses as soon as possible. We must avoid turning TCM's into everyday methods.

Fork in the road ...

6.4 Good riding and training hinges on finding the correct key for each lock we meet. Of course, we could enter by force, and sadly that option is used all too often. This is exactly the critical fork in the road where some approaches part ways from the classical path. Power over the horse is not the goal of the horseman. Rather, a partnership based honestly on mutual understanding and willing participation is the main intent. Only when we approach the horse with dignity, respect and appropriate attitudes, will the creature respond with confidence based on understanding instead of fear.

Discipline

6.5 Discipline is the basis for improvement in both horse and rider. Discipline is a benign, intelligent refocusing and redirecting of energies towards a noble and worthy goal. Discipline has nothing to do with punishment, which should be resorted to extremely rarely.

Kindness

6.6 Fine horsemanship is based on maintaining a kind heart towards horses, and keeping their best interest ever in mind even when, like a child, they may occasionally – *briefly!* – need a firmer moment of guidance. In the end, when discipline is well handled, the truth of their lovely willingness and eager compliance shines through, and we feel deeply moved and uplifted by the heart-warming encounter with the creature's remarkable spirit and generosity (**2.13a** and **b**, **4.9**, **4.18**, **4.44**).

Warming up

6.7 Irrespective of the level of training, horses need to be given time to settle in mentally and physically. An excellent way to proceed for both horse and rider is to begin each session with about five minutes of walk on the buckle (i.e. having the reins at full length, holding them at the buckle) before taking up any rein contact. While walking on the buckle, be sure to ride accurate school figures. Then, a thoughtful warm-up consisting of simple, free-flowing working gaits and large, open school figures is a vital foundation for all work each day again. If we want to enter their sovereign garden, we need to be patient and polite; and to our unexpected joy, the horses will soon invite us in for afternoon tea, because they are curious and gregarious and love the company of good friends.

Repetitions; how many?

6.8 Though a certain amount of repetitive practice may be necessary, prolonged grinding on one exercise is usually not helpful. Fairly frequent changing of rein is also significant, and brings better results than lengthy periods working on one hand. This approach is all part of sound gymnastics that helps develop ambidexterity in both horse and rider. We want, however, to strike a happy medium between doing too little changing, whereby things become stale; and changing so frequently that it upsets the smoothness or consistency of the work. It is also best to avoid working horses more or longer on their difficult or less-preferred side.

Let's dance!

6.9 Horses are natural dancers. They express their exuberant spirit in elastic motion.

Mind – dancing – harmony

6.10 Dancing partners would not find harmony if they were to concentrate solely on each other; that is, aside from feeling a peripheral awareness of each other's presence. But when their minds, their senses, are attuned by an outside harmonizing force – the rhythm, the beat, the expression of the music – a 'third element' outside of them both – they are naturally drawn together to move as one. Similarly, riders should only feel the horse, and think solely of the purpose of their work:

a) Feeling, *counting*, harmonizing with the even, dancing rhythm of the gait (**7.5**, **7.6a**).

b) Guiding the horse on the school figure of choice.

c) Doing some beneficial exercise.

These three points combined represent that third element, that harmonizing influence, drawing horse and rider together. The added bonus to this approach is that it automatically keeps the horse's mind on the work instead of on other things.

Note We want the horse's mind on our **external purpose** (the work) – not on us!

Far-reaching effects ...

6.11 Good work always shows itself by horses reaching evenly and continuously into *both* reins. Forward energy is the key ingredient to achieve reaching. Therefore, if the horse is not reaching, you're likely not driving! In other words, there is not enough energy to cause reaching to happen (but keep in mind **4.49**, **7.20**). Other causes for the horse not reaching for the bit are:

a) The rider's hands are too dominant, hard and uninviting.

b) The horse is driveable but has been dulled by meaningless, nagging leg aids which he ignores to preserve his sanity.

c) The horse is not mentally calm, therefore he is physically tense, reserved, unapproachable. If we drive when the horse is tense it usually results in rushing instead of better stepping, reaching and balancing.

Empty or Lugging

6.12 If the contact is:

a) Empty on both sides (horse comes behind the bit).

6

6.12

b) Heavy or lugging on both sides.

c) When the horse is against the bridle.

The correction for these three occurrences is basically the same. We must animate with the driving aids (equal value on both sides); then rebalance with a half-halt; and then send the horse nicely forward with a giving *attitude* in the contact; repeat as necessary. Riding some transitions can further help lighten the horse into better self-carriage. It is up to the rider to resolve any hanging, heaviness or tensions. 'It takes two to 'hango' (7.7, 7.8).

Not reaching evenly?

6.13 If the horse is lighter on one side, drive him up more with the seat bone (51:50) and leg on that lighter side. While doing so, however, it can be helpful to just *think* of bending the horse around the leg on the heavier side (for details, review 5.25).

Vacillating

6.14 When the horse constantly vacillates between going up against the bit or dropping behind it, the work lacks correct forwardness and therefore balance. Though neither is desirable, of the two evils, it is better to have the horse somewhat against the hand than artificially light behind it.

That compressible feeling

6.15 We want the horse not only to reach for the bridle, but to step up into it, and go forward with it. This has nothing to do with running away against or behind the bit. When the work is right, we get a wonderful, elastic, compressible feeling between the seat and the hand – as though the reins were looped around a large beach balloon – as the horse goes confidently forward.

Inside rein too, please!

6.16 Sometimes the obvious needs to be stated: the requirement of needing to have the horse always reaching into *both* reins equally, implies reaching into the *inside* rein as well. Unless horses continually reach for and gently accept the inside rein as well as the outside one, we have not helped them to come correctly on the aids. A clarification follows.

Inside rein too light? A trick

6.17 To be able to give up the contact on the inside rein for a stride or two, might be considered evidence that the horse is independently balanced and soft to the bend. When this concept is taken to an extreme, however, and we begin to ride whole circles with a slack inside rein, we effectively teach horses a trick through which they learn to contract or reserve their energy on the inside. Here, an artificial bend, carriage and lightness result, as does a subsequent difficulty demonstrating *the* unfalsifiable sign of excellent work: correct forward-and-downward stretching into both reins with the nose in front of the vertical. The rider should be able to ride forward and down at *any* given moment and at *any* level of training (**6.21**, **7.21**).

Readiness

6.18 The goal of good training is to end up having the horse float in a state of back-to-front balance between the seat/legs and the hand (the bridle); and simultaneously be in a state of *lateral* balance and responsiveness between the seat bones, legs and reins. One should feel a constant state of readiness in the horse – that he would, with the subtlest of aids, turn in any direction, or make any transition, up or down, at any moment. Waldemar Seunig called this, 'The blank-cheque state'.

To go, or not to go …

6.19 It is in the skilful balancing between the **go** aids and the **whoa** aids – alternating between the two – that the horse is brought in balance with a high poll and a good, carrying back. This subtle interplay between the driving and receiving aids could be compared to the smooth handling of the clutch and gas pedal in a standard-shift car.

The horse's head position

6.20 The time-honoured criteria for the correct head position of the horse is:

a) The poll must be the highest skeletal point.

b) The face should be at or slightly in front of the vertical.

c) The horse's ears must be on the same level – no tipping.

This standard applies when the reins have been taken up, and the horse is ridden correctly on the aids.

Location of the poll during forward-and-down stretching?

6.21 During forward-and-down stretching the poll will obviously not be the highest *skeletal* point of the horse. What is essential, however, is that the horse's nose (face) remains at, or in front of, the vertical at all times. It must be leading all the way down. This can only come about when the energy connection from the hindquarters to

The author on Barty. Forward and down at the working trot. From Dressage Formula. *J.A. Allen, Imprint of Robert Hale Ltd.* Photo, George Ross.

the bridle remains viable. When forward and down is correct, the horse will remain in a steady, rhythmic gait; he will remain soft through the poll and be in a self-reliant, balanced state. The back will remain up and 'carrying'. And though the neck is stretching downward, the withers will still remain well 'up', being full of impulsive, 'carrying energy'; and the horse will remain nicely in front of the rider's seat and legs through the whole procedure.

It's a billboard

6.22 We could see the position and attitudes of a horse's head and neck as his natural 'billboard' with which he advertises his assessment of the way things are going. However, the billboard can only be a valid guideline for us, when we allow just the horse to write on it. The moment we riders start scribbling on the billboard ourselves, through any artificial placement of the head and neck, the reading of the billboard becomes false. We shut off the horse's honest opinion. We warp his say to hear what we want to hear. When we suppress the horse's vote, we automatically also shut off his natural truth and willing participation. Predictably, from then on everything needs to be forced out of his hide, stride after stride.

Listen? To whom?

6.23 If we are sincere about following classical principles, we would be eager to let horses have their say. Because we could then be genuinely delighted, instead of chagrined or irritated, when a horse points out our weaknesses by going against the bridle, or does not bend, or gets too light and comes behind the hand. After all, if we listen to the horse's instructions and learn to decipher what they are trying to tell us: 'I'm out of balance', or 'My inner energy is unable to engage equally', or 'I can't move freely because of your dominating hands'; or 'The proportion between your hand relative to the amount of energy from your seat/leg is out of kilter', not only would we be learning how to ride properly from true masters, the horses themselves, but it would be a wonderfully inexpensive lesson to boot, much cheaper than attending clinics! We can rely implicitly on one thing: if we become adept at working within the laws of the horses' nature, the creatures will *always* write wonderful things on their billboards. Furthermore, though only very simple work might be demonstrated, the beauty of a horse moving naturally well under a sensitive, harmonious rider is tirelessly enjoyable to experience and to watch: *Beauty of style and harmony and grace and good rhythm depend on simplicity*. Plato.

That coveted shape

6.24 Constant fiddling or sawing with the hands to get and keep the horse's head down in that coveted place, does not belong to worthy horsemanship. Besides deadening the mouth, it ruins the horse's ability to move freely and destroys his desire to contribute. If we learn to direct the horse's energy via his mind – his *understanding* – rather than trying to control his body, he will consequently begin to move his own body and carry himself because of true balance and thus form himself lightly and naturally into that highly coveted external shape. That, and only that, represents honest achievement. It is so dearly important that we dedicate ourselves to search for substantial causes that will bear genuine results, as opposed to chasing after baseless symptoms.

Unintentional: face behind the vertical

6.25 The condition of the horse's face coming behind the vertical with a low poll may occasionally happen to any rider. It should, however, be recognized as undesirable and that it needs to be corrected as soon as possible. The most common reason for this is usually due to the rider's inattentiveness to maintaining adequate energy and balance in a timely fashion. The horse loses impulsion, drops behind the seat and leg and subsequently stops reaching for the bit, the neck shortens and the face comes behind the vertical. This may also occur when initially riding young horses or retraining poorly balanced (or ruined) horses who may rush away on the forehand and barge through the bridle because they have not been helped to understand how to respond suitably to the driving aids and therefore are not balanced and *at* rider's seat and legs. When the rider initially attempts to control such rushing, unavoidably dealing with plenty of weight in the hand, the horse may temporarily overshorten his neck and come behind the vertical. With a little careful training, such happenings can usually be rectified within a very few days.

Deliberate: face behind the vertical

6.26 It is important not to confuse such occasional, accidental aberrations as described above, with riding the horses *deliberately* with a curled-up, short neck, a low poll and with the face behind the vertical (the Rollkur). This has sadly become an integral part of training in some dressage circles. This latter approach is equestrian poison and should be avoided by those who are dedicated to riding in harmony with the horse's nature – by the guidelines of time-honoured classical principles.

Overcoming

6.27 When a horse does come behind the bit (is artificially light, or the poll is low and the face is behind the vertical) this can best be overcome by *lowering* our hands, and helping the horse to reach better up into the bridle with a clear driving aid from seat and leg (supported with a tap of the stick, if necessary) to re-establish a bright, forward-going gait, in conjunction with a good half-halt to maintain the steady rhythm and re-establish balance, after which the hand should have a forward-giving attitude again. A few repetitions of these concepts normally corrects such temporary aberrations, and the horse will then go correctly with the poll high and with his face in front of the vertical. The common error of raising the hand, or giving sharp upward jerks on the bridle, does not address the root of the problem – lack of energy and independent balance. Forwardness and balance, however, can only be achieved with a relaxed, calm horse. It will not work by chasing a tense horse forward in too fast a rhythm. As a complement to the above approach, doing some good, steady, longeing for several weeks (about forty-five minutes per day) can help some horses re-find their own independent balance.

Absorb it ...

6.28 If we feel any 'againstness' in the horse, smother it with passive, non-reaction in the seat. It is an attitude of *neutral*, absorbing diffusion – like a thick, wet slab of clay.

The halt and the half-halt

6.29 During the halt or half-halt we must bring the seat (horse) up to the hand (bit), not the bit back to the seat. When we help the horse to reach correctly for the bridle, he becomes readily haltable with the seat. Take up the halting energy in the seat, via the reins! If response to the halt or half-halt is not crisp, we have likely not adequately helped the horse to come up to the bridle in forwardness. It is worthwhile to reiterate: to avoid dribbling-on halts, think of the brief, clear closing of the outside hand as representing the 'T' at the end of the word 'halt' (**3.29**). Helping the horse to respond brightly to the animating aids is vital to making successful halts and half-halts.

Tech-help

6.30 What should we do with the reins during the half-halt?

a) Confirm the inside rein i.e. have it, so that we do not accidentally bend the horse out, when we;

b) half-halt on the outside rein (active, **close** – o-p-e-n) after which we immediately;

c) give *both* reins *evenly* forward towards the horse's mouth while refreshing the forward energy of the gaits (**5.16d**).

This is a quick sequence, though it takes many words to explain!

Either/or

6.31 For the half-halt: **either** active hand, **or** active leg, **not both** active simultaneously.

Margot Huelke on Lipizzaner stallion Pluto (Pluto III x Bonita III, Temple Farms bred), ca. 1985. Working trot, 10m circle right. Good basic, unified, diagonal movement. Fine, practical position and attitudes of the rider. Photo, Alston Wolf.

F-e-e-e-e-l the walk ooooout

6.32 It is helpful to use our imagination to cause the seat to become the kind of walk we want. If the seat is short and choppy, the walk will likewise be short and choppy. If the seat is long and fluid, the walk will also become long and fluid. Ooooze the walk out. Think of a longer, slower, more active, ground-covering stride – not quicker.

Jigging

6.33 What to do when a horse is tense and jigs at the walk. First of all we must *melt* our seat (extra mozzarella), and gently *ooze* the walk out into longer, smoother strides with the seat and a gentle, broad front line. If it is a serious case of rushing, we need to settle down to the idea of just walking such a horse on the buckle for any number of working sessions, using fairly small circles at first (voltes, or 10m circles maximum), until the horse becomes more trusting and settles down **without us needing to use the reins to slow the pace.** The reins should only be used for simple guidance (neck-reining fashion) during the walk-on-the-buckle exercise. Trying to slow the horse down with the reins, or half-halting is not of value until the horse is calm, accepts the seat and allows himself to be driven. Sharp aids are entirely unhelpful. Endless patience is indispensable to success. When the horse does become driveable again, and *if* he needs to be driven, begin by thinking of gently and *passively* emptying a tube of toothpaste out the front with both legs, while tactfully engaging the seat, i.e. 'tipping the chair'[1] (**9.23**). The use of a few steps of *gentle* leg-yielding may also be helpful to such concepts. Generally, just enjoying the time with such nervous, highly strung horses without having any kind of expectation or agenda will bring better results sooner than any so-called serious training.

Nodding at the walk

6.34 At the walk, the horse's head (ears) should nod **down** to the bridle at each stride; not up towards the rider's head. This nodding down is a sign the horse is beginning to relax and reach over his back to the bridle. Some young, or poorly balanced horses will demonstrate quite a lot of head/neck movement at the walk. Such movement should be elastically followed by the rider's hands and should not be diminished through any artificial means – either by the fixing of the hands, or the use of side-reins or draw-reins. It is damaging to the natural sequence of the walk, and can also negatively affect the other gaits; not to mention causing unsoundness. As the horse becomes more advanced and gains in energy and balance, the head will gradually and automatically begin to be carried more quietly at the walk. When longeing young horses, side-reins should be removed during rest periods at the walk.

1 See Müseler, *Riding Logic*.

Collected trot. Showing fine uphill qualities with great ease, and good, unified, diagonal stepping. From Le Maneige Royal, *Antoine de Pluvinel (1555–1620). J.A. Allen.*

About ghosts

6.35 Any horse will shy occasionally when something startles them. However, when they seem to shy at 'ghosts' or for 'no apparent reason', they are usually showing distrust in the rider's leadership. It is their way of trying to distract us riders away from what we are doing. For example, they are trying to tell us to quit being so serious; to quit staring at their 'fingers' while they work; to quit putting so much pressure on; to quit with the criticism and judgement already! The horse needs to know he has a friend, especially when the chips are down. (For how to deal with startling, see **3.3–3.5**; and how to help lighten up our attitudes when things get too serious, see **8.9, 8.10**)

Just! Keep! Going!

6.36 One of the finest aces up the rider's sleeve is to be non-reactionary to horses' fright, silliness or shying. There is great power in *apparently* ignoring everything. Though we might know exactly why the horse is reacting in a certain way, it is essential not to tell the horse we notice anything. We need to remain serene, and entirely unaffected and **concentrate single-mindedly on the work we intend** (gait, school figure, exercise), and not on the horse or his antics; nor on that which caused the silliness (whether real or imagined). It is the rider's task to set the physical and psychological tone or scene, and through kindness and tactfulness help the horse become calm and trusting – bringing him 'under our tea cozy', so to speak. It can be helpful to think: 'I have all day'; 'I simply don't care'; 'Let's have some fun'; 'Let's you and I do this together' – these thoughts bring ease and playfulness into the partnership. On the other hand, it is fatal to think, 'When is this horse ever going to settle down?'

Diffuse

6.37 When shying happens, deliberately soften the contact and avoid putting more pressure on the horse with the legs. This relaxes the horse, gives him confidence in our guidance, and disarms potential explosions. Tightening the contact or increasing leg pressure ignites the wick to the 'bomb' – guaranteed!

The power of 'small'

6.38 With few exceptions, great accomplishments are the result of many small, ordinary things done well. As the lyrics of a poem by Julia Fletcher Carney, goes, 'Little drops of water, little grains of sand, make the mighty ocean and the pleasant land ...' A magnificent large tree, for example, is the result of countless, patient reproductions of the same, ordinary, little cells. If it is healthy, it will bear fruit abundantly and with great ease. The fruit does not make a large tree! A good, healthy, mature tree produces good fruit and good seed.

Fruit before tree?

6.39 Clearly, excellence in horsemanship is similarly not built by the 'fruit' (endless exercising of piaffe, passage, flying changes, shoulder-in, half-pass, and extensions). It must be built (that is, it needs to be given time to grow) primarily, though not exclusively, on the pure, correct simplicity of ordinary working gaits, good clear transitions, effective timely half-halts, and generally only modest variations in length of stride. Those many small successes help the 'horse tree' to mature naturally and bear some exceptional advanced fruit which will develop easily, if we do not stray from this central standpoint. When simple things are done well, complex things automatically become easier.

The mighty, invisible atom

6.40 There is an old Dutch saying that comes to mind, 'He who does not respect the small is not worthy of the big'.

Discretion – or lemons!

6.41 It is best to take the jewels of extreme extension or collection out of their box only rarely, saving them for special occasions, sharing the joy of them discreetly with others. When cultivated correctly, they are the precious fruit of having patiently developed our own equestrian talents, and having tactfully nourished the gift of the horse's generosity. There is no surer way to sour willing horses than by overpractising exercises which require extreme engagement of their powers.

OK Sparkie! Control – F5!

6.42 While training, we must take great care to preserve the creature's 'horseness'; it is laughably easy to annihilate. In a misdirected search for gaining accuracy and obedience, we can readily turn horses into robots – no more than frivolous toys, a mockery of tricks on demand – unworthy of the noble creature.

Some happy signs …

6.43 A horse's assessment of our work emanates from his facial expressions. On the positive side, the eye appears serene, confident, trusting, spirited and attentive, and the ears, radar-like, swivel back and forth as they listen to the rider or test their surroundings. The mouth chews quietly, the tail is carried and swings gently in time with the movement. When the work is good, a fail-safe sign in our physical feelings is that the horses are easy to sit on, regardless of the degree of collection or extension requested, or the bigness of the natural gaits. This ease is experienced when balance has been well established and the horse's back is properly in play, which causes the rider to be carried forward with the movement. The horse completes the seat.

Physical 'Uh-oh' signs

6.44 **Physically**, when there is disharmony, horses become distrusting and are usually difficult to sit on because the back muscles are tense which causes a false, stiff-legged, jarring or hovering movement and disunited gaits.

Psychological 'Uh-oh' signs

6.45 **Psychologically**, when there is disharmony, we may see two extremes. On one hand, the horses may be excessively jazzed-up, nervy, frightened, or have a wild, angry or unhappy look in their eyes, the ears may be pinned back, the nostrils pursed, the lips snarling, the teeth grinding and unquietness of the tail. On the other hand, the horses may appear quiet but we see the listless, resigned or dead expression in their eyes – the creatures' soul, vigour, and desire have departed, disclosing serious offense against their nature.

No 'art', this ...

6.46 Causing any physical damage to a horse with the whip, spurs, or the bit is utterly unacceptable and indefensible. It is certainly a violation of the noble horse and a serious offense against all that is good and worthy in us as humans. Egon von Neindorff reminded us, 'Where brutality begins, the art desists'.

A Little Anecdote

6.47 Buddha was once threatened with death by a bandit called Angulimal.

'Then be good enough to fulfil my dying wish', said Buddha. 'Cut off the branch of that tree.'

One slash of the sword and it was done! 'What now?' asked the bandit.

'Put it back again', said Buddha.

The bandit laughed. 'You must be crazy to think that anyone can do that.'

'On the contrary, it is *you* who are crazy to think that you are mighty because you can wound and destroy. That is the task of children. The mighty know how to create and heal.'

(Anthony de Mello)

All the qualities of a first class piaffe are present: the horse is beautifully uphill, in front of the rider because of the lowered croup. There is pure diagonal movement and ease and freedom of the forehand. The weight-bearing front leg is correctly vertical, the horse is standing over enough ground. From School of Horsemanship, *François Robichon de la Guérinière, (1688–1751). J.A. Allen.*

CHAPTER VII

Guidelines and Exercises

Dressage is the return of freedom to the horse under rider.

HERMAN KOOPMANS

Introduction

7.0 Training, in the classical tradition, is a conditioning of the horse to help him understand, accept and follow our guidance, doing so as much as humanly possible within the parameters of his nature. Accordingly, our work can only be considered good when it is ratified by the horses themselves as being acceptable. To recap briefly.

Horses demonstrate their approval by:

a) The continued calmness, confidence, and eagerness of their mind and spirit;

b) The impulsive, balanced purity of the three basic natural gaits (the walk, 4-beat; the trot, 2-beat; the canter, 3-beat). The correct way of going is further reflected by the horse's body which grows deep, well-muscled and beautiful;

c) The horse's health, soundness and longevity.

To achieve any measure of equestrian integrity we must hold these simple points as inviolable beacons, the very lodestar for all our interactions with these splendid creatures.

Kenna 1999

Towards this end, the hallmark of good training is made evident by the minimal use of physical energy on our part, and most certainly by the absence of hostility. This does not mean that we should not occasionally assert our leadership with a few stronger aids, should that be necessary (**2.13, 4.9, 4.44a–g**). But such incidents ought to be exceptional and unequivocally brief. When these occasions have been well handled, the horses will go quietly and kindly on smaller, lighter aids immediately afterward. If strong aiding becomes the order of the day and seems to be needed repeatedly or over longer periods, instead of the briefest of seconds, we must seriously question the validity of our attitude and training approach.

Psychologically, if we wish horses to respond to our requests, we need to help them understand. To help them understand we must have clarity of purpose and be appropriate and consistent in our attitudes, aiding and actions. When they do comprehend, they seldom wilfully refuse. If we take these matters to heart and live them faithfully, we will begin to see virtually each horse for the good creature he really is, and how the habit of responding willingly to our guidance, over the months and years of patient training, becomes entirely second nature to the horse.

About the 'how'?

7.1 The success of our leadership lies in always listening to the horses as to *how* to lead them. The good leader motivates without violating physically or mentally.

OPPOSITE PAGE

Above: *Royal Doulton when he first arrived.*

Below: *Royal Doulton about one year later, emanating inner calmness and showing fine muscle development after good care, and appropriate harmonious training.* Photo, Kemra Martin Arias.

Nothing foreign, please

7.2 **a**) Psychologically, the aids must be a clear, reassuring guidance, and not become a 'foreign object' – an offence to the horse's spirit.

b) Physically, excellent balance between the animating and receiving aids helps the horse to know the bit is a friend which he can trust, and not become a 'foreign object' – an offence to the horse's body.

Correct change, please!

7.3 Be prepared for the long haul. With short cuts we only short-change the horses and ourselves.

Not quite so simple, that supposedly simple thing

7.4 All of horsemanship exists in any one of its elements: in the halt; the half-halt; in forward-and-down stretching; in transitions; the piaffe; in the working gaits, and so on. Clearly, if we can not do simple things correctly, we certainly can not do complex things correctly. However, it is far easier to veil fundamental difficulties under the dazzling frills of improvised advanced movements. This leads us to a quote by Angelique Arnauld, 'Perfection consists not in doing extraordinary things, but in doing ordinary things extraordinarily well'.

Key points

7.5 Immediately after 'calm, forward, and straight', the following four points are pivotal in securing consistently good results:

a) maintaining correct tempo and even rhythm;

b) riding accurate school figures;

c) keeping the neck the same;

d) giving forward with both hands equally after each rein aid.

An elaboration of each point follows: (**7.6a** to **7.6d**).

Feel that steady tempo and even rhythm

7.6a We need to make a habit of *consciously* counting a suitable tempo and maintaining an even, steady rhythm for each gait – that is, the tempo we intend, not necessarily the one offered by the horse. 'Tempo' means the rate of, or time between, the beats – slow or quick. This has nothing to do with miles or kilometres per hour. A horse might have a slow tempo at the extended trot, but be moving relatively fast in miles/kilometres per hour. 'Rhythm' means the even continuity or steady repetition of the beats. Some horses have naturally good, deep, rhythmic, balanced gaits. Others, which are not naturally well balanced or athletic (especially when dealing with a rider on their backs), need some helpful intervention to find a suitable tempo and rhythm. We can do so by reciting the following words:

– At the walk, repeat: 'a hundred and twenty-one', 'a hundred and twenty-two'. Say these word slowing and deliberately as each hind leg steps.

– At the trot, repeat: '**one** two **three** four **five** six *se*- ven ...' [1]

– At the canter, repeat: 'ta ta **tummm**, ta ta **tummm**, ta ta **tummm**'.[1]

This continual repetition of the rhythm helps the gait become uniform and predictable – ticking along with clockwork steadiness. It is an essential part of helping horses find relaxation and balance. One of the signs that we are succeeding is that the footfall of the gaits becomes pure, energetic and ever more quiet. As for the rider, it is important to have a relaxed, resting seat and position, which should continuously participate and flow harmoniously with the horse's movement. Riders who are musically inclined will find it easier to maintain a good, steady 'dancing' rhythm and suitable tempo (3.8).

1 This way of counting the trot and canter rhythms originates from Egon von Neindorff.

Crystal clear school figures

7.6b The clarity of purpose in choosing the kind of school figure, its exact size and location is central to our leadership. Besides helping us, as guardians of the riverbanks, to discover where the water (horse's energy, balance) is seeping out, it also quietly, imperceptibly and effortlessly draws the horse to our purpose and results in harmony. School figures can be any of those commonly recommended in most riding texts or prescribed for competitions, or they can be invented. That which determines a school figure's usefulness, *besides the vital aspect of giving the rider clear purpose*, is that it should help in the gymnastic development of the horse (**4.17**).

No wobbles here

7.6c It must be our highest priority to **keep the neck the same**, that is, **laterally absolutely stable, quiet and steady** onto the withers and shoulders, especially during:

a) *any* guiding aids;

b) half-halting or halting, and reining-back (**5.28**, **5.30**, **5.34**).

Accidental changing of the neck is a major cause for poor directional control and loss of alignment and balance. **Incorrect, one-sided rein aids are often the cause for such problems.** Lateral stability of the neck should not be achieved by any form of rigid fixing of the hands. It is established through correct forwardness, balance and small timely corrections (**5.2–5.6**, **5.35**). Forwardness stabilizes the neck, the gait and the direction.

About reins like rods

7.6d It is equally important to have a clear forward-pushing *attitude* with **both hands equally** most of the time – especially after any rein aid. This allows the horse's shoulders to be carried freely in the buoyant forward energy of the gaits. Egon von Neindorff recommended thinking of pushing a tea trolley forward in front of us. Others have painted the excellent mental picture of the reins being like two rods which we push forward. None of these ideas necessarily implies the need to push the hands forward measurably, nor to lose the contact. It is the attitude, the clear forward-allowing intention which is most significant. One may of course give measurably if one wishes to – when lengthening the stride, or when deliberately riding forward-and-down stretching (**6.17**, **6.21**, **7.19**, **7.21**). To achieve this giving attitude, think of the forearms as being hollow tubes through which we allow forward energy to flow to the bridle. Or think of the energy as flowing underneath the forearm through the little finger to the horse's mouth.

Ludwig Koch. Piaffe. Showing ideal uphill qualities and excellent balance indicated by the vertical weight-bearing front leg.

Feathering

7.7 Feathering can be used when bending presents a challenge. It is a fine way of effortlessly dissolving tensions or the horse's leaning on the *inside* rein. One could say, it takes the wind out of the horse's stiff-side sails. It works because we give the horse no support on the inside rein – a dead, hanging or holding against the horse's leaning. He therefore *automatically* begins to use his less-preferred outside hind leg more. Both hind legs are therefore more evenly in use. The horse consequently begins to reach more evenly into both reins (**5.40**, **6.8**, **10.7b**, **10.11**).

How to feather

7.8 Feathering is done by quickly (almost abruptly!) releasing or softening *only* **the fingers** on the inside rein. The contact is softened **without losing it!** It is important *not* to let the whole hand or arm go forward. After this abrupt softening, then *gently and slowly* return the fingers to where they were before the release. Take about one second to do so (count, 'twenty-one' *slowly*). The concept of feathering is completely defeated if, after the release, the rider closes the hand forcefully, thinking in terms of having to *make* the horse quit the hanging, or to *make* him yield to the bend. On the other hand, giving too much on the inside rein (either in amount or duration) is also unproductive as that would cause the horse to start bending outwards. Feathering is most effective when the rider sends the horse nicely forward and thinks predominantly of the inside leg and the *outside* rein. Through this the horse becomes soft and even in the reins, and bending becomes a non-issue. The bending request on the inside rein should be strictly limited to the amount that the horse follows easily and *willingly* (**2.12**, **5.7**, **5.13** and **Note** in **5.34**).

Important Only use feathering when the heavier rein is on the *inside* (**4.28**). It is not useful to feather on the outside rein when it is heavier (a half-halt would be wanted here).

Duckies in a row

7.9 *In conjunction with adequate forward energy from the inside leg*, it is the duty of the rider's outside seat bone, leg and rein to line-up the horse to be straight; i.e., single-track work (**10.8**). The horse's *outside* shoulder is aligned within the stream of energy, so that his head, neck, shoulder, body and hindquarters are aligned and become **one piece**. This is essential for achieving independent balance, and counts especially when riding in the direction of the horse's hollow side. 'One piece', or 'one chunk', in no way implies stiffness or inflexibility in the horse. It just means that we need to think of addressing the horse as a unit, not a series of independent, unrelated parts (**5.29**, **10.35**).

Fifty-fifty ...

7.10 Normally, the seat bones should have equal weight in them: 50:50 (3.13). When deliberately increasing the *emphasis* on one seat bone (when bending, changing direction, or cantering on, for example) then we should think of having 55:50 weight distribution during the brief moment of aiding. In other words, we should *not* lighten one seat bone in order to put extra emphasis in the other one. Seat aids are all a good deal more subtle than is generally appreciated. As with all aiding, this greater emphasizing of one seat bone should always be temporary: stop giving the aid immediately after the desired effect has been achieved; return to 50:50.

Horse higher under one seat bone?

7.11 What can we do when a horse's back is higher under one seat bone? This usually occurs in combination with the horse being uneven in the reins. Besides the need for serenity and patience, the success of the following recommendation depends on the rider's ability to remain truly central and independently balanced, despite the horse's unevenness and crookedness (review 3.13). That which is possibly hard to understand (and harder yet to explain!) is that our *influence* needs to remain even (same concept as 5.28, 5.30). Yet we need to accept *passively* the horse's unevenness under the seat. The solution is to be found indirectly, by allowing that steady, *passive*, increased pressure under the high-side seat bone to remain while we walk the horse on a circle (from volte to 10m, not larger) in the direction of that high side. The naturally occurring emphasis (extra pressure) of the seat bone on the horse's high side should *not* be lessened. Nor should the lighter weight in the seat bone on the horse's low side be increased in an attempt to make the weight in the seat bones even. That would only cause us to lower ourselves to the horse's crookedness and unevenness and would nullify the opportunity of having the horse's own intelligence partake in the solution (3.27). It is important to stress, however, that although one seat bone is lighter, it should nevertheless always to be in contact with the saddle!

As we persist with the circle work, in due time (usually within 10–15 minutes) the horse will begin to soften his back on the high side because of that steady, unyielding inside seat bone presence, and will then also automatically begin to raise his back up better under the lighter seat bone. This in turn makes it easier to animate the hind leg on the lighter side whereby the horse will also begin to take a better, more even contact on the lighter rein. The quieter (the more passive) the reins are during this entire procedure the more readily the horse will begin to respond to the passive seat influences. Whether or not there is an immediate improvement when doing this exercise, it is important to quietly persist with the circle work and to change the rein about every 5–6 circles. When riding on the hand where the horse's back is lower, it is important to have very little bend – or even no bend at all – in the body/neck, until there is better evenness under the seat and in the reins. This whole procedure encourages equal use of both hind legs and generally results in improved balance and forwardness. As an adjunct to these recommendations, it may be found useful to ride ribbon candy serpentines (**5.16**).

The power of passive

7.12 Seemingly magical pathways open when we discover how to awaken the horse's willing participation. One way to achieve this is to learn how to set up steady, *passive* circumstances or parameters, such as those described in **7.11**, and then let the horse figure out how to make himself comfortable within those circumstances. Horses learn best from lessons which they teach themselves. All the rider (or person longeing) needs to do is keep an accurate school figure and judiciously attend to forwardness. Though such work may seem simple, to be successful it is essential to remain consistent and focused on clarity of purpose.

About fairness and fatigue

7.13 The treasure of the horse's willing participation can best be cultivated by remaining fair and consistent in our expectations, that is, working within the limits of each horse's level of fitness and training. It is especially crucial to be modest in how much we ask for when things go *well*. If we fail to rest horses *before* fatigue sets in, and continue instead to make more demands, they will be justifiably less prone to offer their energies to us willingly in future. The same holds true if we ask for work which is too advanced, we can expect horses to begin seeking self-protective evasions. As usual, we are the dummies, and the horses suffer. It is a lose-lose situation.

Note It is equally important for riders to work honestly within their own actual level of ability and experience; and not to over-reach at the unfair expense of the horse.

Turtle and hare

7.14a Good riding is based on consistently striving to let the horse's actual state of development determine the course and the rate the training will take. If, in extreme cases, that means needing to hack a youngster or a spoiled horse on the buckle in the countryside for several months, so be it (again, on the buckle means to ride with a completely loose, given rein, held only at the buckle). If, when training a sensitive or 'hot' horse, it means careful building of canter and counter-canter, doing only simple changes of lead, even for several years before doing flying changes, so be it. To further underscore this concept: even when there are no apparent complications during training, it is wise to leave a horse at the same level for one or two, sometimes even three months, before proceeding with new or more advanced exercises. It is just like breaking-in a new pair of riding boots. Though one can, of course, pull them on immediately, it will nevertheless take some time before they become truly comfortable.

Flying changes?

7.14b The main ingredients:

a) Take the time to develop consistently good, relaxed, balanced canter departs from the walk on both leads.

b) Develop solid, predictable, relaxed counter-canter.

c) Be absolutely relaxed in seat and position.

d) Change your leg position *one stride* before you want the horse to change his lead, as you say to yourself – in time with the canter rhythm – 'first me, then you'.

e) Simply allow the horse the freedom to change without any further aiding influence.

f) Practise sparingly.

Doing what's right

7.15 For the horseman no work is too menial or rudimentary, and piaffe is not treasured above a *good* working trot. Delight is gained within modest requests, based in the rider's respect for horses and a genuine desire to guard and foster their spontaneous willingness above all. Through this approach we are granted the joy of experiencing the glorious feeling of harmony and playful ease in our riding.

In the tool box

7.16 A useful instrument in the trainer's tool kit is to, in effect, longe the horse from the saddle. However, as opposed to actually using a longe line, surcingle and side-reins, all this means is to keep the work very simple, just ticking along steadily on large school figures (especially, large circles) at the working trot. This applies particularly when working young horses or retraining spoiled ones. The simplicity of such work brings rich rewards. But, as with so many things that are supposedly uncomplicated, it requires an experienced rider to do them well. Much of our human thinking tends to be altogether too busy and complex; and when combined with impatience and having difficulty living in the present moment, the concepts just mentioned usually accrue only indifferent results.

No 'cookie cutters' here

7.17 Success lies not merely in doing recommended exercises, but in how and when we do them. Patterned, cookie-cutter methods become stale and mechanical all too soon. Besides being inflexible to the needs of the living moment, they readily cause horses to anticipate. We need to remain feelingly and mentally agile, ever ready to come up with a fresh approach. See guidelines for aiding **4.16, 4.23, 4.25, 4.51**.

... over the fence!

7.18 A concept commonly used in jumping can be usefully applied to all riding: 'Throw your heart over the fence and go after it'. Our 'heart' is our desire, our conceptual resolve, of wanting to go **there** purposefully. For the dressage rider this imaginary, ever-receding focal point should be well ahead of us (15–20m or more) and we must want to go after it continually. Horses recognize such clarity of purpose and usually respond favourably. It is worthwhile to reiterate: *feel* the horse under you, *think* only of what's *out there*. Do not think of the horse! The horse will automatically become a useful *extension* of our mind when we, in a matter-of-fact way, trust the horse to follow our guidance by thinking strictly of our external purpose. (Also see **4.12, 4.13**). 7.18

Jiji Melon eventing on Dante. Irrespective of the equestrian discipline we choose, all the principles apply. Here we see the rider's heart and mind clearly engaged towards her 'external purpose' resulting in excellent dynamic harmony. Do not think of the horse! Feel the horse under you! Think only of your purpose – think 'out there'! Photo by Lawrence.

About blossoms

7.19 Correct forward-and-down stretching is like a spring blossom which patiently contains the fullness of the autumn harvest. Forward and down encourages the extensors and flexors to pulse evenly and harmoniously, leading to a good tempo, an even rhythm and purity of the three basic gaits.

Paramedics, please

7.20 In riding, the horse's 'reaching' can be equated in importance with breathing. When the horse stops reaching for the bit, horsemanship stops breathing. Call the paramedics! The 'paramedics' are the rider's animating influences which resuscitate the horse's desire to reach for the bridle again.

On the buckle at any time

7.21 When things are right, the rider will always be able to walk on the buckle, even immediately after sparkling collected work, and have the horse walk on absolutely calmly, stretching his head and neck effortlessly downward, completely unconcerned about the preceding work. Another highly revealing clincher is to be able to ride a good, solid forward and down (nose at, or in front of the vertical) in any gait, at any moment, at any level of work. It is an unfalsifiable proof of the pudding. Anyone can force horses' heads down into place. But correct forward-and-down stretching can not be falsified. It requires the entire training system to be built patiently on a correct foundation. See **6.21** for an elaboration of correct forward-and-down qualities.

A thankful heart

7.22 Let us not wait until things go perfectly before we praise the horse. Praise does not say to the horse, 'This is perfect'. Praise says, 'I appreciate you, thank you for that better response!' Indeed, *appreciation* is the nub of the matter! Horses are completely unconcerned about their owner having just spent thousands on saddles, bridles and blankets, or on stabling, veterinary or shoeing expenses. They respond to the priceless gift of being appreciated. Therefore the qualities of **recognition** and **gratitude** are central to fair and viable leadership: recognize even the smallest response from the horse and express *genuine* gratitude. Lack of gratitude or appreciation smothers willing responsiveness – the horse's natural, childlike desire to please (**4.44**).

No debts here ...

7.23 Truly, it is essential to realize that horses owe us absolutely nothing, ever! Considering they almost invariably go well when we ride well, it should be clear that we need to let the rays of our benevolent heart smile on our horses frequently, patting them gently and encouraging them often during the ride, 'Come, let's do this together, you and me. Good boy!'

A little anecdote

7.24 I once had a student who had a serious case of non-stop fiddleitis with her hands. It was such an ingrained habit that she was entirely oblivious of doing so. Though sincere, conscientious, constructively self-critical and hard-working beyond reproach, she had a devil of a time getting those hands quiet. To help her become more aware, I had to remind her countless upon countless times. I explained, reasoned, encouraged and, in my inimitable way, *emphasized* over and over, and prodded yet again – all seemingly to little or no avail. I finally got so tired of having to do this interminable repetition that something had to be done. Indeed, as the old cliché goes, 'Necessity is the mother of invention'. And thankfully it was. I got a little bell, and every time those hands moved I would ring that bell. Well, needless to say, it rang an awful lot at first; and my student got more and more frustrated as time went on. This proceeded until she suddenly pulled her horse up short in front of me, and exclaimed, 'I can't wait to win the "no-bell" prize!'

Sally Cleaver's Andalusian stallion, Banbury Sampson. A wonderfully impulsive extended trot showing exemplary, natural, uphill balance – sheer exuberance in motion! Despite the enormous forwardness, take note of how the front knee is bent, and the front hoof does not pass the line drawn down the horse's face to the ground. This indicates that the horse's back is properly engaged: the horse is a beautiful, supple, relaxed unit. Note the natural, poll-high carriage and the nose in front of the vertical. Nature knows best!

CHAPTER VIII

Inspiration for Animation

The essential premise for training is the psychological connection between man and creature. When this is lacking, the rider cannot cultivate or ennoble, but only enslave.

Col. Hans Handler,
former director of the Spanish Riding School.

8.1 Who among us hasn't smiled in amazement watching horses out in pasture strutting their spectacular stuff; and wished we could recreate and experience such grandeur while riding? To fulfil such a dream may at first seem like an imposing challenge. However, I believe it is possible to find some promising ways of approaching this goal, if we carefully analyze the essential ingredients which spawn that delightful movement in the horse.

8.2 In the list of the most important elements to achieve our objective, the horse's forward desire is unquestionably at the top. The old Masters repeatedly identified forward energy as the very lifeblood of horsemanship – indispensable for achieving balance and ultimately the liberation of the horse under saddle (**6.0**).

8.3 How can we possibly set about the task of animating in the right way?

Surely, a good place to start is to observe the horse's own natural tendencies and to analyze the differences between horses at liberty and those under saddle. That which strikes me first is horses simply know best how to move their own body! Truly, their Creator has imbued them with the very best ability to move themselves. It is essential that we trust in that implicitly and allow them to do just that – though we may at times need to remind them to use that talent a bit more liberally!

8.4 What ignites that exhilarating movement which causes the horse's whole body to take on a more beautiful, unified form? The answer surely lies in the creature's highly impressionable nature. Horses are great enthusiasts at heart and are readily stimulated by the tenor of their surroundings – which includes the rider. When excited by circumstance, energy bubbles up irrepressibly from their remarkable spirit which impels that magical dance to float forward with elastic ease.

8.5 We can deliberately tap into the horse's delightful openness to suggestion by calling on the power of our own creative enthusiasm! In other words, we can succeed in sparking our horse's natural ability to express himself by becoming his motivational speaker! Just as we can hardly resist an infectious laugh, or find it hard to sit still when hearing a bouncy tune, so too the highly impressionable horse will almost always want to partake in the excitement of the rider's catchy new game. Isn't that how horses set each other off? One rambunctious youngster high-blows, kicks-up his heels and sets the whole herd galloping off in a playful frolic. It seems patently impossible for them to resist joining in on such electrically charged moments. (**4.8**, **4.11**)

8.6 Though we may have developed a talent for inspiring energy with our enthusiastic motivation, we may still need to back up our natural animating aids with the stick or spur. For most horses, an occasional little tap-tap reminder with the stick, or prick-prick from the spur is sufficient to evoke adequate forward energy. However, when *initially* helping to encourage lethargic or seriously dulled horses to muster up a better response to the forward aids, a clearer, more direct approach may be needed. In this case, it is critical to be absolutely consistent and unwavering in our level of expectation and to use the stick or spur *briefly* and effectively – literally, for no more than a second. It is important to keep in mind that aggression or unfairness extinguish the horse's willingness to participate. We want to plug into the horse's delight, not into his fight or flight (**4.9–4.11**, **4.44–4.47** and **7.22**).

8.7 The subject of animating may seem out of place when dealing with very sensitive or nervous horses. Nevertheless, it is equally important to learn how to tactfully convert the tense, brittle energy of such horses into smooth, elastic forwardness. In such cases our inspiration must first come in the form of trustworthy, calming leadership. This helps soothe the horse's mind and brings him under the security of our 'tea cozy' – that comforting arm-around-the-shoulder quality. Animating influences are viable only once the horse is truly relaxed and driveable. Tense or nervous rushing should not be confused with true forwardness. But once high-strung horses do become calm and trusting, they usually also become quite lazy. Thoroughbreds often display this trait. Thus the inspiring animation mentioned above becomes equally beneficial in such cases. It remains our prime challenge to fit our approach to the needs of each individual horse and to grow with them as they develop (**4.49**, **4.83**).

8.8 By understanding the horse's own natural tendencies and channeling them discreetly, we raise our work to a more dignified, worthy level. As leaders we contribute intelligent, disciplined structure and benevolent purpose to the partnership. The horse is then able to contribute his physical energy and exuberance. Approaching riding in this way makes for a more rewarding and joyful experience for both horse and rider.

Related material

4.9 – The power of small
4.41 – Responding because of understanding. (Good energy)
4.42 – Reacting because of coercion. (Poor energy)
4.43 – Belly to belly?
4.44 – 'Tuning': acceptable versus unacceptable – the details.
11.28 – The pure performance

11.29 – Shooting for what?
11.31 – True learning
11.32 – Holier than thou

A Little Anecdote

8.9 A mother was observing her child at play with a friend, when a quarrel broke out. At first she thought to leave them work it out for themselves. But, after some time, she decided to see if she couldn't possibly help resolve their differences. Tactfully she intervened, suggesting they play a new game. The game entailed that they could say whatever they wanted to each other, but that it should be done in the following way. They were to substitute the vowels in every word with just one other vowel of their choice. Well, out it came! 'Yii tiik mi criyins ind briki ini!' (You took my crayons and broke one!). As they got better at substituting the vowels, there was only giggling and uproarious laughter to be heard. The anger and frustration vanished and friendship ruled once more. It was splendid![1]

A spoon full of levity ...

8.10 When frustration rises and things get a bit too serious in our riding, one might apply the above concept. Just try telling your horse with a straight face, 'Whin I siy whii, I miin whii! Ind whin I siy gi, I miin gi!' ('When I say whoa, I mean whoa! And when I say go I mean go!?') As inner smiles take over, things will go remarkably better . Your horse will also be smiling, and thanking you.

1 Concept heard on a German morning radio program (SWR).

Piaffe. Egon von Neindorff on Andalusian stallion Juca in the piaffe. A centaur, demonstrating an exemplary connected seat and position — a seamless part of the horse's energies. Photo, Prof. Ulrich Schnitzer.

CHAPTER IX

The Seat: Prince of Riding Instruments

9.1 To talk about the seat means to talk about all of horsemanship – a total influence, a mastery of self, a philosophy of riding encompassing respect for the horse, and a comprehensive understanding of his nature. Because the body mirrors the spirit, inevitably each rider's seat is suffused with the character, temperament, personality, mood and desire – the very essence, colour and flavour of their soul.

9.2 Studying the workings of the seat, an elusive quantity at best, can be compared in certain ways to the modern-day study of sub-atomic particles. Just as these can only be partially understood through their interactions and effects upon other elements and forces, so too the seat can only be understood through its effects, with which it is wholly entwined, on the horse. One can certainly establish fairly good approximations of how to attain satisfactory results from the seat/position. But it would be a staggeringly futile undertaking to explain in detail the myriad seat adjustments required during any one riding session, these being relevant only to that particular horse, rider and moment in time. Only personal experience on many different horses can begin to divulge the rainbow of nuances meaningfully to each rider.

9.3 The purpose of this chapter is to present an outline of those practical conditions under which correct seat elements can develop. It is only when such development has taken place that an effective influence can be brought to bear by the rider, this in turn resulting in a living state of harmony with the horse.

9.4 Fundamentally, it is the seat's function to transmit and receive all messages. But the seat itself is the message! It must therefore constantly be drawn into a ribbon of accord, reeling off harmoniously and articulately as the horse moves.

9.5 It is a paradoxical and somewhat disconcerting fact, considering the great effort required to develop an effective seat, that ideal harmony is actually a gift of circumstance, and comes to the rider only in small, jewel-like moments over the years. This is so because harmony between two living creatures can not be dictated, but must be willed to come about by each participant. At best we can strive to make circumstances such that harmony has the greatest chance of occurring.

9.6 Though certain technicalities must be mastered before a good seat can evolve, ideal seat attitudes are a result of intuition and automatic reactions which must be roundly served by adequate, correct experience. This might be compared to the development of a goal keeper's skill, who through accumulated experience and intuition, and not just reflexes, narrows the chances of being scored against. Sensitivity, keen intuition, and correct habits can equally give the rider the best opportunity to react suitably to any given situation.

9.7 For unspoiled horses, and those without complex temperaments, response to the influences of a *correct* seat is virtually inescapable. The horses instantly recognize and respect it. This is so because correct signaling from the seat addresses the natural forces of physics, affecting the very nub of the creature's make-up – his sense of well-being and self-preservation – his balance. Horses are, after all, master physicists! It is one of the foremost goals of horsemanship, however, that not only horse and rider be individually balanced, but that their centres of balance should coincide. In this synchronized state the rider's slightest influences come right home, their effects being strongly amplified, whereby the rider can start to 'play' the horse effortlessly at the tip of their seat-wand. The horse becomes subject to the rider, and the rider subject to the horse; neither can any longer make any motions without fully taking into account the other.

9.8 The horses are masters at communicating via subtle physical gesture; to them it is simple foal's play, they do it all the time. It is little wonder they can perform so beautifully to the 'invisible' seat aids. Yet, before the rider can enter into this world of fine-spun communication, the seat must become quiet, free of tensions, or any unintentional movements in the saddle.

9.9 See note below.[1]

9.10 To attain the basic quietness, balance and independence of the seat can take an able-bodied rider about three years, provided one has had correct guidance. However, assimilating a viable, rich equine vocabulary, and an articulate mode of expression – cultivating an educated seat – is a never-ending task which can always be honed. Furthermore, it is essential for the aspiring rider to develop suppleness, agility, and physical fitness, without which quality horsemanship is unthinkable.

9.11 There are three inseparable prerequisites that constitute the seat:

a) The rider's position.

b) Control over the attitudes of the lower back and pelvis.

c) The ability to help the horse to arrive at a supple, balanced, 'carrying' state. The horse completes the seat!

9.12 The first two points will be covered in detail here. The last point will not, since it entails the full spectrum of working the horse, many aspects of which are described throughout this volume.

9.13 To elaborate on the first prerequisite: the purpose of the rider's work on their position must be the achievement of functionality through the deliberate placement of all body parts into the most favourable attitude. In this way balance and control of the horse can be achieved with minimum physical effort on the rider's part. If the rider's seat and position are correct, the horse will have the best opportunity to go correctly.

1 Concepts previously placed in 9.9 have been merged in other sections where those concepts have been expanded.

9.14 There are no short-cuts for the initial hard work, nor any skirting of the pains which must be endured in acquiring a viable seat and position. Those who believe that one can first learn to get the horse going, and only later paste on a pleasing position artificially, are doomed to failure. Without the major work-tool of a *functional* and correct position, the rider is left no choice but to resort to false influences which become ingrained habits, very hard to eradicate later. Such contrived influences have little impact on the natural forces of the horse other than to disrupt them. Only through the initial technical correctness of the position is the potential for effective aiding established.

Ludwig Koch. Travers left. Collected trot. Simply perfection.

9.15 Going to the opposite extreme, however, of concentrating solely on position correctness to the exclusion of constant, analytical sensing of its effects on the horse, can only fashion an irrelevant, ineffectual 'glass-cabinet ornament', which must some how be maintained despite the jarring motion of the horse.

9.16 The next prerequisite concerns achieving correct attitudes of the lower back and pelvis. These are vital to excellence in horsemanship. Egon von Neindorff often reminded us, 'The seat is the conductor of the orchestra.' Its effects are aimed singularly at achieving accurate control over the tone of the aids, doing so by adjusting the attitude of the fall of the rider's weight into the seat bones. This, in turn, intimately affects the direction and flow of energy through the horse's body. Though these attitudes have a decisive impact in the giving of aids, the actual physical alterations in the rider to affect these weight influences are minute – virtually imperceptible to the observer. They become quite useless when exaggerated. It is a powerful, yet subtle, tool!

9.17 The greatest problems in learning what 'driving' (animating) and its phantom partner 'bracing the back' is all about, lies in the tendency, so often the case, to latch onto some isolated highlight of theoretical advice, and all but ignoring the finer nuances which are at least as, if not more, important. This results in large distortions of what was originally perfectly sound advice. Riders end up looking like bear-wrestlers, with backs hunched, chests collapsed, stomachs pulled back, and not infrequently leaning back while the seat is shoved forward-and-under exaggeratedly. They literally try to ram their horses forward, physically, stride after stride, with gross, active gyrations of the pelvis in the saddle. Not only are these attitudes unsightly, but their forceful nature actually prevents the horse from using his powers freely. These are certainly not the elements of grace and effortlessness which mark the valid classical seat.

9.18 The absolute pinnacle to which the rider should aspire is to develop a seat/position which is in living harmony with – absolutely quiet relative to – the horse's back. Any additional active motion in the rider is most undesirable. Certainly, rounding the back, or leaning backward with a 'pushing' attitude, reaps no positive benefit at all. These misunderstandings of what driving is lead to the following complications:

- a lack of independent balance of the upper body and hands
- being left behind the motion
- hanging onto the horse's mouth
- forcefully trapping the horse between the seat/legs and the hands.

9.19 The notion that one needs to drive continuously is also erroneous. The rider must learn to generate a certain, necessary level of impulsion, enough to achieve balance and fluid forward motion (i.e. helping the horse come correctly on the aids), and then delegate the task of maintaining that energy level to the horse. The rider then, as administrator, only needs to monitor the horse's performance and, when necessary, rejuvenate the forwardness with short, energetic driving aids, just sufficient to remind the horse to uphold his end of the bargain.

9.20 If the seat is incorrect, the energy level depletes readily (imagine a leaky car tyre.) The necessary 'pressure' in the horse, that is, the inner energy of forward desire and balance, can not be maintained, and must be regenerated time and time again. This is both needlessly tiring and wholly ineffective riding that can only produce dull or soured horses. Unless the quality of the seat is improved the rider will be forced to resort to excessive use of stick or spurs, resulting in a vicious cycle of intensified and multiplied giving of aids; instead of ideally causing the horse to respond to ever fewer and lighter aids. Ask a bit, get a response, coast a bit! **Let the horse do the work! Delegate!** (4.45–4.47)

9.21 Though most novice riders can be helped to find a pretty good position fairly quickly, it takes many years of practice before the suitable essences – true energy patterns – begin to develop and flow correctly and naturally through their bodies; that is, for the seat/position to become true. Irrespective of the level of talent, there is simply no substitute for years of experience.

9.22 We must take it as a basic premise that during riding our muscles should be used with supple contractions and relaxations. Any hard cramping or spastic contraction, contortion, or stiffness anywhere in the rider's body is most undesirable, and are a major impediment to correct influences. However, suppleness or relaxation does not mean sloppiness. Think 'elegance'!

9.23 During any driving or bracing, our body energy pattern is brought into play by broadening the front line; 'tipping the chair'; riding the horse and hips through the elbows; riding the chest through the shoulders; and kneeling (3.15). These various ways of describing what the seat and position do are actually just **one single influence**, like a small orchestra. They could also be described as:

a) **drawing** the horse forward from the front line (like a spinnaker drawing a sailboat through the water) and/or

b) **urging** forward from the lower back without in any way altering the pelvic tilt.

Again, **a**) and **b**) are one and the same thing, though stated differently. (In vain, one tries to describe the undescribable. For better or worse, it can only be experienced with the horse as living reflector.) The seat bones continue to be held nicely forward by pelvic tilt, **but the focus of the energy while bracing lies in the passive, forward pushing energy of the small of the back** (*not* to be hollowed), **and/or drawing forward from the navel area.** Furthermore, the forward urging of the horse is *not* done with the seat bones themselves. They are merely 'implements of transfer' which automatically come into play from the correct effects of **a**) and **b**) above.

9.24 To draw an analogy: a car's tyres transmit energy to the road. But the energy comes from the engine which is located elsewhere, and only a good suspension can keep the tyres securely connected to the road. So too with the seat bones (the tires), though they do transmit the energy to the horse, the forward influence (energy) comes from the navel and/or from the *top* of the pelvis (the engine). And it is only through the correct attitude of upper-body posture, in combination with suitable lower back and hip qualities (the suspension), that the seat bones remain glued effectively on the saddle at all times. From this we can see that the bracing or driving should in no way alter the outward appearance of the rider's body or position. Regardless of how much such aids are emphasized, the seat must always remain quiet and resting: relaxed, elastic and harmonious with the movement of the horse's back (no cramping or stiffness).

9.25 Slight bracing/driving influences could be seen as the *physical* aspects of the 'shadow' or 'maintaining' aid, and might be used more or less continuously; as long as the horse remains driveable, and his back compliant. Not only is such bracing/driving an essential part of such a small encouraging influence, but it helps the seat remain glued seamlessly to the horse's back. It is indispensable to our participating with the horse's movement, that is, to achieving harmony such as would exist between dancing partners: not so much presence that it is disturbing; not so little that one has to be dragged along like a rag doll. (See **3.1**, **4.89c**, **7.6a** regarding participation; and **4.53** for the mental aspect of the shadow aid.)

9.26 **Bracing** (it might better be called 'engaging the seat') is to be employed with sensitivity and discretion, the rider always listening to the horse in order to measure the exact amount that might be necessary and acceptable as each moment requires. Stronger bracing influences which might be used, for example, while tuning the horse to the animating aids in conjunction with rebalancing half-halts, should be used only *very* briefly (**4.44d**). Also, when used during half-halts, the duration and intensity of bracing should be commensurate to the amount of 'receiving' needed in the reins at any given moment (**3.24**). It should last only as long as that receiving, or taking up, of the energy is necessary, seldom more than a stride – after which the seat/position should immediately flow freely with the horse's forward motion once again.

9.27 As with all things one must find the happy medium. When the back is braced too briefly or softly, it will not help the horse to respond adequately to the desired 'gathering-up-under' effect during the half-halt. Used too long or too strongly, its effects could be negated because the horse can readily learn to drop his back or stiffen against the rider (instead of becoming better balanced and more springy in his hindquarters) in order to free himself from such an overbearing, unyielding influence. When properly understood the whole half-halt procedure is a very brief, subtle, yet effective influence.

9.28 The interplay between the three main seat/position attitudes,

a) neutral, 'flowing with';

b) maintaining; and

c) bracing, is as follows.

Bracing is used during rebalancing half-halts (during which time the reins may take on a sustaining, receiving attitude); and the maintaining or flowing-with attitudes are applied in-between the moments of aiding (during which time the hand must assume a forward-allowing, giving attitude again (**4.39**).

Thus to recap briefly:

9.29 a) **Stretching** the position produces the rider's carriage or bearing (grow tall, think of elegance). It consolidates the body's energies and gives the rider a practical, useful form. It facilitates control over the weight and balance. It is used *gently* most of the time, but is emphasized during halts, half-halts, transitions, or when tuning to the driving aids, balancing, or putting the horse on the aids, etc.

9.30 b) **Pelvic tilt** causes the seat bones to point more or less emphatically forward. It is achieved by flattening the lower back – the lumbar vertebrae. An indispensable part of this is to fill and stretch the nape of the neck *gently* into the back of the collar (**3.18–3.20**). Pelvic tilt should in no way impede our ability to flow with the horse's movements. It causes the forward emphasis to be transmitted to the horse more from the back of the seat bones. Yet, the source of the forward-urging/drawing energy pattern comes from the top of the pelvis (where one's belt intersects the spine at the back) and/or from the navel. It is used more or less most of the time, and assists the rider in keeping the horse in front of the seat and leg. This too is briefly more emphasized while driving, and during halts, half-halts, and transitions. Pelvic tilt is only an *inner* attitude, or an inner energy adjustment, within the rider's body. It is not externally visible. Furthermore, it should not cause the rider to raise the pubic bone off the saddle, nor to collapse the front line, nor to lean back. And, finally, it is a steady quality, and should not cause the pelvis to wobble stride after stride (belly flopping).

9.31 c) **Bracing the back (engaging the seat)** has a balancing/collecting/engaging effect on the horse when used in conjunction with **a**) and **b**), and with the appropriate half-halt (sustaining, or receiving, or taking up of the energy) attitude in the reins. During halting or half-halting, bracing is a momentary stilling or waiting effect of the seat/position which gives the reins the necessary *elastic* base to be able to take up or receive the forward energy the horse brings to the bridle and converts it into balance. It could be said that the rein energy becomes directly connected to the lower back via the elbow during bracing. **This influence should be used only *very* temporarily!**

9.32 As long as we recognize these three major seat functions as being individual aspects, and learn to orchestrate them harmoniously, then, in time, success will be ours. Physically and technically, the correctness of the seat and position influences should be measured by the continued **purity of the gaits**. Psychologically, our influence must always be ratified by the horse – his acceptance being demonstrated by his continuous **mental serenity and calmness** (6.43).

9.33 It is important to note that throughout this chapter only the actual seat and position aspects have been discussed. However, it is essential to reemphasize, that **the seat's influence must be seen as a purely *passive* one** – though very real and extremely important. If the seat's passive influences do not elicit an adequate response, the rider's active leg aids need to come into play. These may, of course, be backed up by the stick or spurs, should that be necessary. The leg aids tune the horse to respond to the seat; the stick and spur aids tune the horse to respond to the legs (4.44).

9.34 Those aspects of horsemanship that are a deeply hidden mystery to those who have not been exposed to refined equestrian study, become plainly self-evident to the rider who has achieved self-mastery, and has taken the time to cultivate a high-quality seat and position. The years of ardent work finally surrender their most cherished fruit: the liberation of the horse under saddle. The creature, sensing the freedom of his powers – being entirely uninhibited by the presence of the rider in the saddle – begins to carry the rider with graceful ease upon his supple, elastic back, buoyed-up on the cadenced movements of his independent, balanced gaits.

9.35 In achieving these results, the rider senses a deep, unspeakable delight in experiencing true harmony with another living creature. It is a home coming – the ultimate prize, secured by the skilful use of this prince of riding instruments: the seat.

The Author on Barty. Half-pass (travers) left. The rider is sitting a bit too deep to the left. Photo, George Ross.

CHAPTER X

Two-track 'Ins and Outs'

10.1 The main purpose of this chapter is to present a detailed study of the various single- and two-track gymnastic training positions for the horse. It describes their purpose, their influence on the horse, how and why they work, and the sequence in which to use them for best results.

10.2 When used in the manner described, these positions will be found to be of great value in fortifying a rather commonly found weak area in the training of so many horses that lies somewhere between the early introductory work of the young horse and the point at which the more advanced training can proceed. Clearly, it is best when training develops smoothly and seamlessly, which it can, if we always let the horse's actual ability and level dictate the speed at which we proceed.

10.3 The work described below is entirely in accord with, and encompasses, the six basic training guidelines (rhythm, relaxation, contact, straightness, impulsion, collection), and is a safe, practical and systematic medium within which these can be successfully developed.

10.4 One of the greatest benefits gained from the appropriate use of these positions is that they assist the rider to gain systematic and unforced access to the giving of the horse's hindquarters: i.e. the deep bending or flexing of the three major joints – the hip, stifle and hock. This results in the lowering of the croup which gives horses the desired uphill quality in their way of going. This element is indispensable for achieving correct collection (10.25–10.29).

10.5 We will be starting the work described below under the premise that the young horse has already been kindly started (not before four years old); that he has been properly longed for six to eight weeks (4–5 days a week for about 20–30 minutes per day), and is now under saddle, content to carry the rider. It is essential that this initial phase has been well laid down. It has little value to begin with the stages presented below until a degree of steadiness has been achieved, especially improved basic control over guidance on simple, large school figures at the walk and trot.

10.6 As a part of the introductory training just mentioned, it is also useful to do some turns on the forehand (*sparingly,* to prevent looseness of the hindquarters), and a little leg-yielding. These two exercises are not really to be considered part of the gymnastic effects that will later be achieved through the proper use of the single- and two-track phases described below. They are useful, however, to initially help the young horse understand lateral responsiveness to the rider's legs. When judiciously used, two-track work in general is also useful for the rider to learn how to coordinate the aids; especially with regard to gaining control over straightness and alignment.

Important points to consider

10.7 I ask the reader's forbearance, as there will be some patience needed with the following admittedly copious details. But, since the devil is in the details, they will be found useful to any serious student of the horse. The following general information applies to all the stages.

a) Accurate riding of the school figures is vital to success. Two-track work can only bring reliable results when we can position the horse accurately **relative to the line** (school figure) on which we have chosen to ride. Sloppiness regarding school figures can only lead to indifferent results.

b) During all work we need to change the rein fairly frequently, about every 3–4 rounds of the school; or 4, 5 or 6 times around a circle. It is best *not* to work the horse more on his difficult or less-preferred side! See **6.8** regarding frequency of changes.

c) For horses who are physically awkward or very one-sided, at the rising trot it can be helpful to switch the diagonal on which we are rising, without changing the rein, irrespective of on which hand we are riding. Change the diagonal every 6–10 strides or so; the frequency of switching to be adjusted to the horse's needs.

d) The normal infusion of variety in the work is important. The work can always be freshened-up with a little canter, but only if the youngster doesn't become tense, unsteady, or fussy.

e) It is wonderful to use the forward-and-down stretching exercise as part of the daily work.

f) We need to keep in mind a suitable balance between work and rest periods during any ride, and to schedule adequate days off work as well as days spent hacking outdoors. Physically tired or mentally soured horses don't learn much, other than ways of evading work.

g) Any time we run into difficulty while going to any of the higher stages described below, we should simply spend a little more time in the previous stage(s) until the horse is more solid in that work: When in trouble, do less! Brief trial runs (literally just a few steps) can always be done in the higher stages to test the water, so to speak. That is likely a good policy across the board, whenever proceeding into areas which are new to the horse or rider. When things go well, continue for only a *little* while longer (20–30 seconds) then rest and praise the horse. At all cost, avoid grinding. Do exercises with measure so the horse does not get an aversion to the work.

What is the difference between single-track and two-track work?

10.8 – Any work is considered **single-track work** as long as both hind legs track anywhere *within* the dual paths made by the two front legs (see Stages I, II and III below).

– In **two-track work** the forehand and hindquarters each travel on their own separate paths, hence 'two' tracks; this is irrespective of whether the horse's *individual* legs make three or four separate tracks. Thus, only when one or both hind legs are *deliberately* made to track to the *outside of* the dual path made by the front legs, would the work be considered true two-track work (see Stages IV, V and VI below).

– Correct two-track work should not be confused with unwanted, accidental crookedness.

Note Before going into the specifics of the various single-track and two-track positions of the horse, it is highly recommended that the reader review the essential points about the rider's leg position (**5.20–5.23**). Likewise, review the time-honoured standards for the horse's head position (**6.20**). It is essential these criteria are closely adhered to. It is especially critical to avoid the horse's head/ears tipping during two-track work.

10.9 In summarizing, despite the fact that no two horses, riders, or circumstances are alike, it is recommended that the stages of this guideline be followed in the order they are given. The only variation in the work from horse to horse would lie not so much in rearranging or skipping stages but, depending on the horse's talents or difficulties, one would spend more or less time at any given stage before proceeding to the next. Let's begin.

STAGE I

Straight riding: The swinging-leg phase. (Figure 10.1)

10.10 – Ride forward.

– Use mainly rising trot.

– *No bend,* anywhere!

– Line up the **outside legs**.

Main goal To stabilize the young horse through forwardness and straightness. This is the first step in establishing control and stability over the hindquarters relative to the forehand through **mechanical** straightening, using diagonal aiding in forwardness, whereby the horse's energy can begin to be deliberately directed. Through the use of a steady, rhythmic, forward gait the horse learns to reach for the bit, and begins to accept both reins more evenly. (For more on diagonal aiding see **4.70, 4.71, 10.14.**)

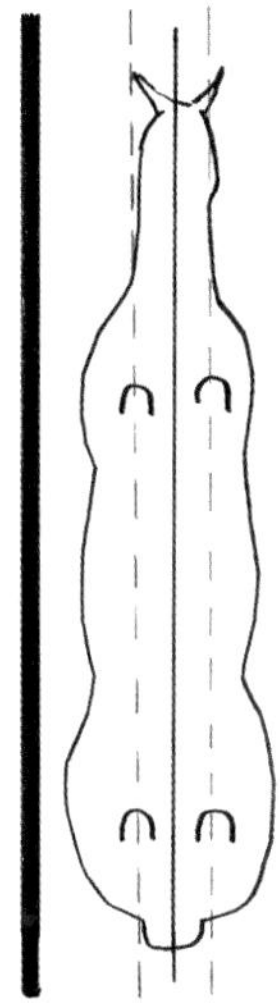

Figure 10.1

Crookedness

10.11 Most horses, like humans, are one-sided. This is simply a natural preference of one side over the other. This causes the horse to want to avoid loading his less-preferred hind leg by going crooked (he evades by going *outside* of the dual path made by the front legs **10.8**). As a result the horse also loads the diagonally opposite shoulder/rein more heavily. Crookedness is *not* a disobedience. It is a natural avenue for saving the less-preferred hind leg. The rider can *help* the horse overcome this lateral imbalance through straightening in forwardness which is developed by this first phase. This helps the horse find better balance by gradually engaging both hind legs more evenly (**7.7, 7.8**).

Detailed description

10.12 In this first swinging-leg phase we must keep the horse's **entire spine absolutely straight**, no bend anywhere. 'Swinging-leg' means the horse moves freely forward without any particular degree of impulsion or collection in the gaits. We must ride forward, full school (5.37), preferably at rising trot, and line-up the horse's **outside legs** (those closest to the wall). For example, on the right hand in the school, align the left shoulder (left front leg) with the left hind leg. **Keep the neck straight!**, absolutely straight, especially at its base, and accept quietly, patiently, and steadily, any unevenness (extra weight) the horse might put in one of the reins. *Do not* half-halt, fiddle, or muck about with the heavier rein, and especially don't try to bend the horse with the rein on the stiff or heavy side.[1] Why? There are several reasons for this.

a) It does not address the cause of the one-sided heaviness (less preferred hind leg).

b) Attempts at *active* correction of a symptom, without addressing the cause, only put the horse's mental and physical powers *actively* against us, which is much worse than a bit of temporary passive leaning on one rein.

c) Half-halts can only be properly understood by the horse once he has learned to accept the drive, reach for the bit, and come on the aids from behind.

10.13 The only viable, *long-term* solution is to, 1) keep the neck straight; 2) accept the heavier rein passively and quietly; 3) **send the horse forward!**; 4) align the horse's outside legs with a diagonal aiding influence, to produce a **mechanical straightness**: leg on the side of the evading croup – rein on the side of the evading shoulder (4.74). A truly resolved **dynamic straightness**, which encompasses the even, balanced loading of the horse's legs throughout all school figures and exercises, is approached only over years of patient gymnastic work.

1 We certainly may help the horse to bend in his body through the correct positioning of our legs, but that comes into play more in the next stage.

10.14 If necessary, to achieve this mechanical straightness we may *initially* need to put whichever of our legs back as much as necessary on the side of the evading croup. For example: when riding on the left hand in the school, if the horse's croup swings in to the left, and the shoulder presses right, out towards the wall, we may put our left leg back, and feel (be aware of) the diagonally opposite right rein in order to *passively* align the horse's right shoulder in front of his right hind leg. During such aligning, it is essential to maintain the straightness of the base of the neck. Furthermore, do not try to achieve straightness by pushing the hindquarters over to line up behind the shoulders. That only produces fishtailing or looseness in the quarters. Instead, think of the diagonal influence (leg *active* if necessary – for energy; rein usually *passive*) to realign the shoulders in front of the hindquarters. Crookedness is best corrected in *forwardness*, rather than in a sideways or lateral manner. In the above example, the rider's right (outside) leg may *temporarily* need to be placed in the forward 'inside' position (for explanations see **5.23–5.25**, **6.3** and *Figure* 10.3 page 162)

10.15 The overall success of this phase comes only by forward riding without rushing the horse. We must keep an even rhythm, and a pace just a bit stronger (more ground covering, *not* quicker in tempo) than the horse might want to offer on his own. This kind of work is like longeing from the saddle (**7.16**). At first it might take from 30 to 45 minutes before the horse begins to use his less preferred leg. We will feel this happening as the horse begins to seek less support on the heavier rein, and becomes more even in both. As this becomes more habitual, day by day this evenness in the contact will come a little sooner. Further, the horse will also simultaneously begin to yield at the poll (*never* to be forced by the hand) and to chew on the bit. It is the first rudimentary step of coming on the aids. Only time and patience bring home the real product.

10.16 Concepts previously placed in 10.16 have been merged in other sections where those concepts have been expanded.

10.17 *If* the horse becomes steady at remaining straight most of the time, and loads his hind legs more evenly, made evident by the nice even acceptance of both reins, we can then proceed to the next phase. Depending on the horse, it can take anywhere from a few weeks to several months to achieve this. With the use of this straight work, as with all things, the happy medium is always best. Though wobbly young horses with skinny, loose necks would initially gain from doing this work, if it were done too long with well-balanced, athletic youngsters, they could become ungainly or laterally stiff. Again, so much depends on the experience and talents of the rider, and the degree of difficulty presented by the conformation, temperament, and sensitivity of any given horse.

STAGE II

Bend while going straight (Figure 10.2)

10.18 – This is *single-track* or microscopic shoulder-fore.

- This is *not* yet two-track work.
- Bend must be introduced mainly in the body.
- Continue to align the outside legs while bending.
- Continue to use straight lines as much as possible. Once familiarity and stability are established, then circles can also be ridden in this position.
- When used on straight lines this could be considered just a hint of the **first phase, or type of bending: bend and move** ***away from*** **the bend.** This is more clearly indicated in Stages IV and V.

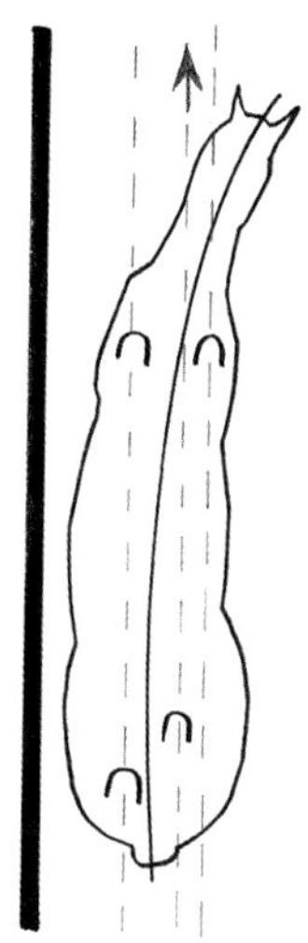

Figure 10.2

- Once consistency is established, the counter-exercise may also be used (**10.21**).

Main goal To teach the horse to bend in his body while maintaining the straightness of his tracking on the school figure and the continued even acceptance of both reins. It is the first inkling to help the horse to understand and accept the outside rein and leg.

Note 1 This position can be safely used for the bulk of the work until the horse is adequately prepared for the next stage. It is important to repeat, this is *not* two-track work!

Note 2 It is the subtlety of these positions that is the key to their success. More angle is *not* better!

Application

10.19 By increasing the weight *slightly* in the inside seat bone (51:50), leg and stirrup, and by the appropriate placing of the rider's legs (inside leg close to the girth, outside leg approximately 4–5 inches back [see **5.20, b!**]) we invite the horse to bend mainly in his body. We need to take care to bend the neck only very slightly, especially avoid bending it at its base, by keeping the shoulders well contained between the seat bones, knees and reins (**5.7**). The reader will perhaps already have foreseen the potential danger that can occur while we shift our legs to achieve a bend in the body. The horse could very easily become crooked again by bringing the croup in, instead of bending while continuing to track straight. Therefore patience in these first stages will pay off in large dividends later on. We may need to go back and forth repeatedly between Stage I and Stage II, so that, when the bend is introduced, we do not unintentionally have the horse become crooked again – that is our responsibility, not the horse's! (**4.27**).

10.20 It is critical that we initiate the bend while continuing to keep the horse's outside legs aligned. This is the steady, all-important constant on which we must build our training and by which we can judge the speed at which we may progress in these earliest phases. If we can, **a**) manage to keep the outside legs lined up, and **b**) keep the horse stepping evenly into both reins while bending, then among the great benefits of the bend-while-straight work is, just because of this bend in his body, the horse will *automatically* begin to travel with his inside hind leg closer to the outside hind leg. The inside hind leg will therefore also automatically track between both front legs. As is commonly known, good balance can best be fostered when the hind legs begin to travel closer together. This wonderful exercise helps us to start bringing about that requirement.

Counter-bend while going straight (Figure 10.3)

10.21 Once the above work has progressed to the point where the horse allows himself to be bent while maintaining all the necessary criteria mentioned above, *then* we can introduce the single-track counter-bend while going straight. The outside legs (relative to the bend) are to be lined up. We must take care to guard against the croup swinging loosely into the school, or towards the wall. Also, the counter-exercise should only be done on the long sides of the school, not yet on the short sides, through the corners, or on circles at this stage of the training. Remember to switch the diagonal of the rising trot during such counter-exercises.

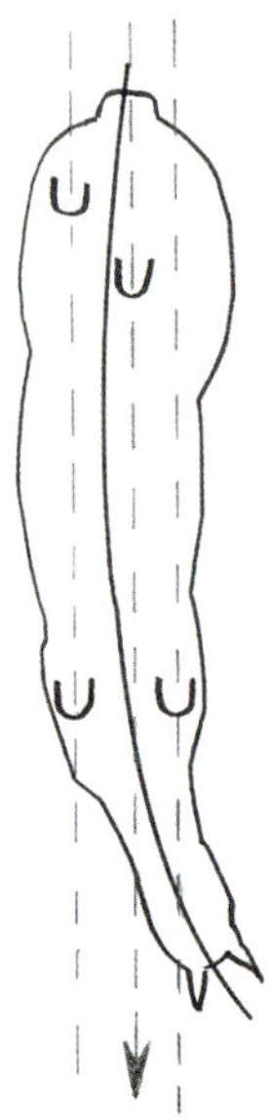

Figure 10.3

10.22 Only if the horse can go easily in the single-track shoulder-fore, and its counter-exercise while,

a) Staying aligned with his outside legs, (relative to the direction of the bend); and

b) Continuing to step evenly into both reins, on simple school figures (full school, across the diagonals, and large circles) without tending to crookedness or becoming heavier on either rein;

then we can safely begin with Stage III, and start lining up the horse's **inside legs**. A word of caution: there are potentially considerable dangers in starting too early with the next phase because the horse's stream of energy or alignment, can only be easily and correctly contained once the horse has correctly learned to understand and accept the outside rein and leg (through adequate preparation in the first two stages). He must also have learned to carry his shoulders more evenly in the balanced energy of both hind legs. These would be signs of correct lateral and longitudinal balance. If we were to line up the inside legs prematurely, the horse's outside shoulder would all too easily fall out. The rider would have no recourse to prevent this, other than by using *inappropriate* forcefulness with the outside rein/leg. The horse would consequently load that loose outside shoulder more heavily, and bore on that outside rein yet more; thus affording the rider very poor control over the energy, balance, and straightness (**4.33**, **4.34**, **5.8**).

OPPOSITE PAGE

Right: *The author riding thoroughbred mare Lady. Counter shoulder-fore at the working trot. The horse is bent left while going on the right hand in the arena. The outside legs (the horse's right legs) are aligned. The inside (left) hind leg travels exactly between the path of the front legs. Note that, though the horse is bent left, the rider's right leg is forward. The reason for this is as described in section* **5.23–5.25**. *Also see* **6.3**, *about temporary corrective measures.* Photo, Alston Wolf.

STAGE III

Bend in while going straight (Figure 10.4)

10.23 – This is a microscopic croup-in or travers. It is commonly known as 'position', that attitude which the rider will be using for most work from here on (if a bend in the horse is wanted).

– It is *not* yet two-track! It is still single-track work.

– The horse must remain even in both reins, while now staying lined up with the **inside legs**.

– Because of the bend in the body, (as described earlier in Stage II) the hind legs will continue to travel closely together, only this time the **outside hind leg** will be traveling on a path between the two front legs.

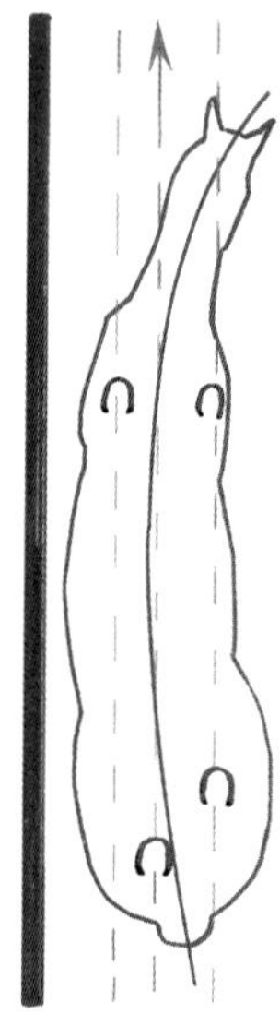

Figure 10.4

Begin to teach the horse this work on straight lines. When this position is ridden in *single track* on a circle it constitutes the **second phase, or type, of bending: bend, and move** *in the direction* **of the bend** (*Figure 10.5*, A-2 and B-2).

10.24 It can not be sufficiently strongly emphasized the importance of working on straight lines while *initially* teaching the horse how to bend his body while keeping his inside legs lined up. Why? Because it is easier to control the straightness of the horse's travel on a linearly straight line, and thereby gain and maintain the accurate direction of the energy from the hindquarters into both reins. Usually, once such control on straight lines has been well established, will the transition to riding this position on curved lines be more easily and successfully made.

Addressing the bending or flexing of the three major joints of the hind legs

10.25 Once this work can be transferred to circles or curved lines without causing lateral crookedness, then this Stage III position becomes the first avenue through which we can *deliberately* begin to affect the amount of bending (flexing or compression) in the joints of the hind legs. Let's see how this works. (*Figure 10.5*, A-2 and B-2.)

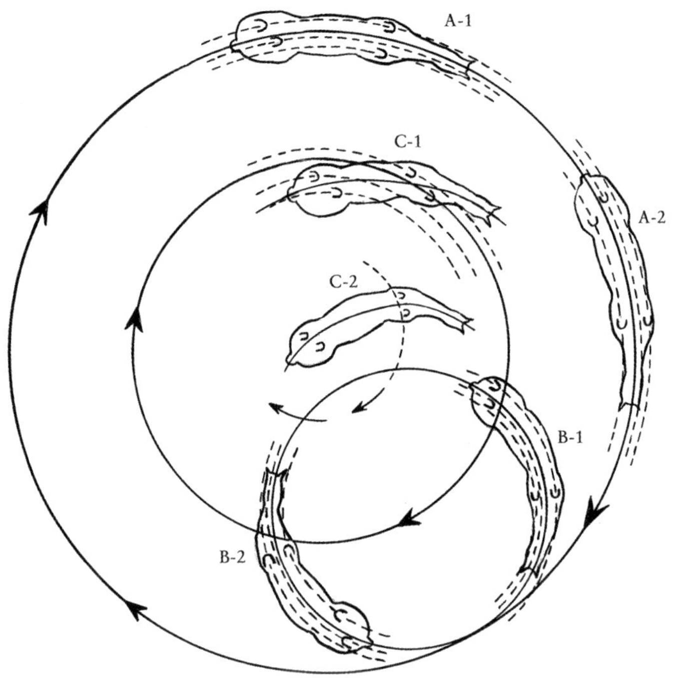

Figure 10.5

Figure 10.5 Circle work. At A-1 the horse is shown in single-track work on a large circle with the outside legs aligned. The same in B-1 but on a small circle. In this case the inside hind leg travels under and across the horse's body. Here the joints of the inside hind leg will not be as prone to flex or bend as when the inside legs are aligned (A-2 , B-2). When the inside legs are aligned, then the smaller the circle the more the inside hind leg is addressed to make shorter higher steps which results in greater bending or flexion of the three major joints – a prerequisite to correct collection. C-1 shows the horse in two-track work with the croup-in on the small circle. This could be developed into a turn on the haunches, C-2.

10.26 When traveling on a circle with the inside legs lined up, the inside legs travel a shorter distance than the outside legs. If the horse expends the same amount of energy with both hind legs as he should (made evident in that he remains even in both reins), then the inside hind leg will use up that extra energy by bending its joints more, resulting in a higher, rounder stride. The outside hind leg will continue to make a somewhat longer and flatter step. The smaller the circle the more we would need to bend the horse's body (to maintain the same bend in the spine as the arc of the curve being ridden) and the more the horse would subsequently have to load and flex the joints of his inside hind leg. By contrast, the horse would hardly feel the need to flex the inside hind leg while doing this position on straight lines.

10.27 Choosing a suitable size of circle for the horse's level of development is therefore important, so that we do not overbend or overload an ill-prepared horse. We should introduce these concepts so gradually that the horse remains unaware (through stress, fatigue, or pain) that his hind legs are being bent or loaded. Overfacing here is indeed most counter-productive, because we would readily teach the horse how to find self-protective evasions.

Using force to bend hind legs

10.28 If a horse has been forcibly trained, the above-mentioned benefits will not show themselves. This applies in particular to those which have been forced into a head position with hand-oriented training. When the horses are hauled together into an artificial frame, crammed between the seat/leg and hand, the hindquarters will tend to stiffen, rather than flex or bend elastically and lower. The supple bending in the major joints will not occur. This is true regardless of either the amount of bend in the body, or the *supposed* suppleness that might have been achieved through the commonly implemented lateral overbending or see-sawing of the horse's neck with the hands; or overbending with the face behind the vertical: the chin-on-chest Rollkur. Both are injurious to the horse's wellbeing. Such misdirected influences only achieve slackness in the neck, reserved forwardness, and not a supple horse at all. True suppleness is only achieved through energetic forward impulse which liberates the horse's body because of improved balance.

10.29 Steinbrecht, in his book *Gymnasium des Pferdes*, warns us that, if we try to coerce the hind legs to flex through forceful means, not only will we most assuredly fail to achieve our goal but the horse will likely end up breaking down in his hocks, and/or in his back (tying up, spasms of the loin muscles) because of this. These are certainly common 'diseases' of some dressage horses. To view rare black and white video of riding at the *old* (*circa*1935) Spanish Riding School which shows horses going correctly uphill with deeply bent haunches, see the Google search detail on page 3.

General comments

10.30 Most of this Stage III work should be done in a good, forward, rhythmic, working trot. Alternate between sitting and rising trot. Change the rein reasonably frequently, giving each hind leg time to work/bend/load as an inside leg, and then to rest (relatively speaking) as an outside leg. Again, do *not* spend more time on the horse's less preferred side. Use some forward-and-down stretching to assure continued elastic suppleness and 'aliveness' in all the muscles, and therefore fluidity in the gaits. Give reasonable work/rest cycles. Don't overpractise, especially when the horse starts to get the idea. Endless grinding only sours horses, whereby they become less willing to offer the rider anything on their own.

10.31 At this point transitions, half-halts, halts, turns on the haunches, some rein-back, and small variations of lengthen/shorten strides, gradually become more and more useful tools. Moderation is the key to success. Remember that transferring the weight to the hindquarters can only be successful when the hind legs are bent (flexed) unforcedly and easily. And, when they do begin to bend, avoid becoming greedy and end up overloading them, either by spending *too much time* in collection, or by *overcollecting* (overcompressing) at any given moment. Hurry up slowly! Things can turn sour very quickly. Through alternating judiciously between moments of putting greater stress on the hindquarters by using smaller circles and, on the other hand, freeing the horse up with more open working gaits on large school figures, we can experience how to balance out the forward-pushing impulsive energy, with the flexing/loading, collecting energy.

Note It is also a useful exercise to practise riding the Stage III attitude on straight lines and alternating that with the occasional circle or volte; in the same fashion as described in *Figure 10.8* on page 172; doing so, in this case, without the shoulder-in angle along the long side.

10.32 *If* the horse plays along easily with the requirements of Stage III, we can proceed with the next phase. How do we know? The horse will be bright and eager when he sees the rider coming with the saddle and tack the following morning! The horse will readily accept the work and remain even in the reins, the gaits will remain pure, fluid, elastic and rhythmic through all the work. The back will remain easy to sit on.

STAGE IV and STAGE V

Two-track shoulder-fore and true shoulder-in[2] *(Figures 10.6 and 10.7)*

10.33 – True two-track work begins here.

– The shoulders are brought yet further into the school, going through a four-track phase (correct two-track shoulder-fore, *Figure 10.6*, with each leg tracking on its own path) just before arriving at the desired goal of true three-track shoulder-in, with the inside hind leg tracking exactly in the path of the outside front leg, *Figure 10.7*.

10.34 These positions/exercises confirm the horse yet more clearly on the outside aids, and solidify the balance and suppleness. They help increase the lateral bending in the body, which leads to a yet greater bending (flexing) of the three major joints of the hind legs. They are therefore a viable means to develop higher degrees

2 Before going into true shoulder-in, it will be found worthwhile to review the comments about leg positioning (5.20–5.23)

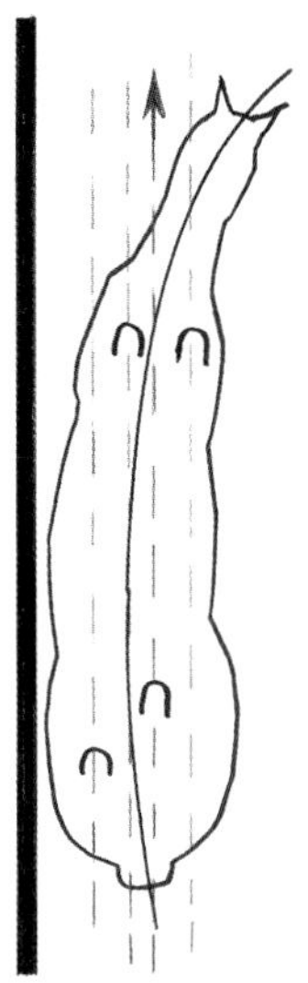

Figure 10.6

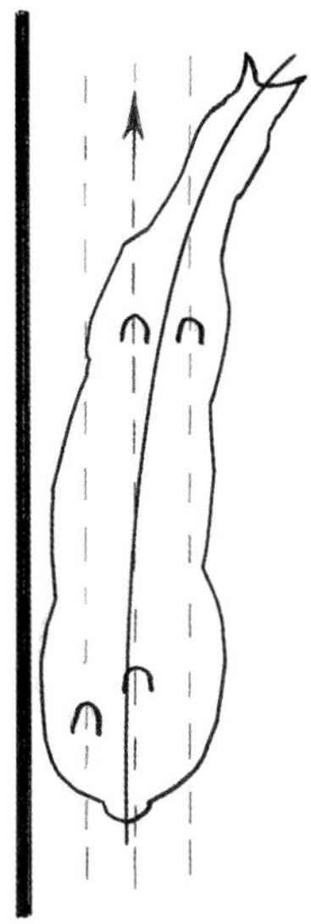

Figure 10.7

of collection. Do not overbend the neck laterally, especially at its base. The counter-exercises can be usefully implemented once the 'normal' shoulder-fore and shoulder-in have been well established.

10.35 Begin the exercise by riding a single-track volte at the beginning of the long side, then flow into the shoulder-in angle along the wall (*Figure 10.8*). Strange as it may seem, it is best *not* **to think** of shoulder-fore or shoulder-in as being two-track work! This usually only gets the rider into an unhappy 'sidewaysing' of the horse. Initially, it may be found helpful to practise riding the shoulder-in *angle* without any bend at all, just for a few minutes as a temporary exercise, to come to understand and feel what the correct energies of a shoulder-fore or shoulder-in are like (especially learning how to control the outside shoulder and maintain independent balance). Keep the perception of the horse as remaining **one chunk** from head to tail, absolutely straight in his neck and body, while riding along the school wall in that three-track shoulder-in angle (**5.29, 7.9**). Once this unified quality has been adequately experienced then, while keeping that feel and understanding, begin to do the exercise with a bend. A yet more advanced and worthwhile exercise is to do shoulder-in on a large circle. However, great care must be taken to avoid the common errors described in **10.36**.

Note It is important always to look through the horse's ears, even during two-track work.

Common shoulder-in errors

10.36 Using the above concept of practicing the three-track shoulder-in angle, while *temporarily* alternating between riding it with or without a bend, helps the rider get away from the following common shoulder-in errors.

- Overbending the neck, cracking it off at the withers (**4.77**, *Figure* 4.1).
- Trying to shove the horse sideways by jamming the inside rein against the neck/withers (see common misuses of the inside rein **4.78**).
- Shoving the horse sideways with the inside leg (instead of the inside leg doing its actual most important job of providing forward energy as needed – which the *passive* outside leg shunts to the bridle – and the outside rein then uses that energy to place the shoulders to the inside. After all, the exercise is called 'shoulder-in', and not 'shove the horse sideways!'; nor 'push the croup out!').
- Falsely achieving the exercise by putting the inside leg back towards the horse's flank or croup, resulting in a poor form of leg-yielding – or 'croup-out' (**5.22**).
- Looking up the wall of the long side during shoulder-fore and shoulder-in, instead of continuing to look through the horse's ears, in harmony with the direction of the bend.

These aberrations cause a stopping-up of the horse's forward energies by restricting the free movement of the inside hind leg which leads to poor quality, broken-apart gaits.

10.37 It is important to know that shoulder-fore and shoulder-in do not of themselves cause greater bending (flexing) of the hind legs. Instead, they are exercises, or positions, which besides assisting in furthering overall suppleness of the hindquarters and greater responsiveness to the rider's weight and leg aids, give us access to greater lateral bending of the horse's body (especially *behind* the withers), which in turn, **when ridden as single-track work on bent lines, in Stage III mode**, causes the joints of the hind legs to flex more, lowering the hindquarters. This quality is then taken into the following work and exercises; at first for only a few strides, but with time and care it begins to suffuse all the work. In other words, they are accessing exercises or door openers. This is why it can be productive to alternate between riding the two-track shoulder-in up the long wall, and converting this directly into single-track 10m circles or voltes at various intervals on the long sides of the school (*Figure 10.8* page 172). The greater lateral bending in the body gained during the two-track shoulder-in work is immediately converted into greater flexing of the joints of the inside hind leg while on the single-track circles. Back and forth between these two modes is the key to success (in moderation, of course!).

Summarizing shoulder-in concepts

10.38 If we were to take the shoulders yet further into the school we would begin to head into leg-yielding angles (four-track shoulder-in, *Figure 10.9*); and normal leg-yielding at approximately a 45° angle relative to the line being ridden, *Figure 10.10*. These variations are not necessarily incorrect. Horses usually gladly move more sideways away from the rider's leg, but are not as challenged by that greater angle (beyond three tracks, that is) to flex and engage the hind legs. Leg-yielding emphasizes lateral responsiveness. The three-track shoulder-in emphasizes suppleness, bending, engagement and collection.

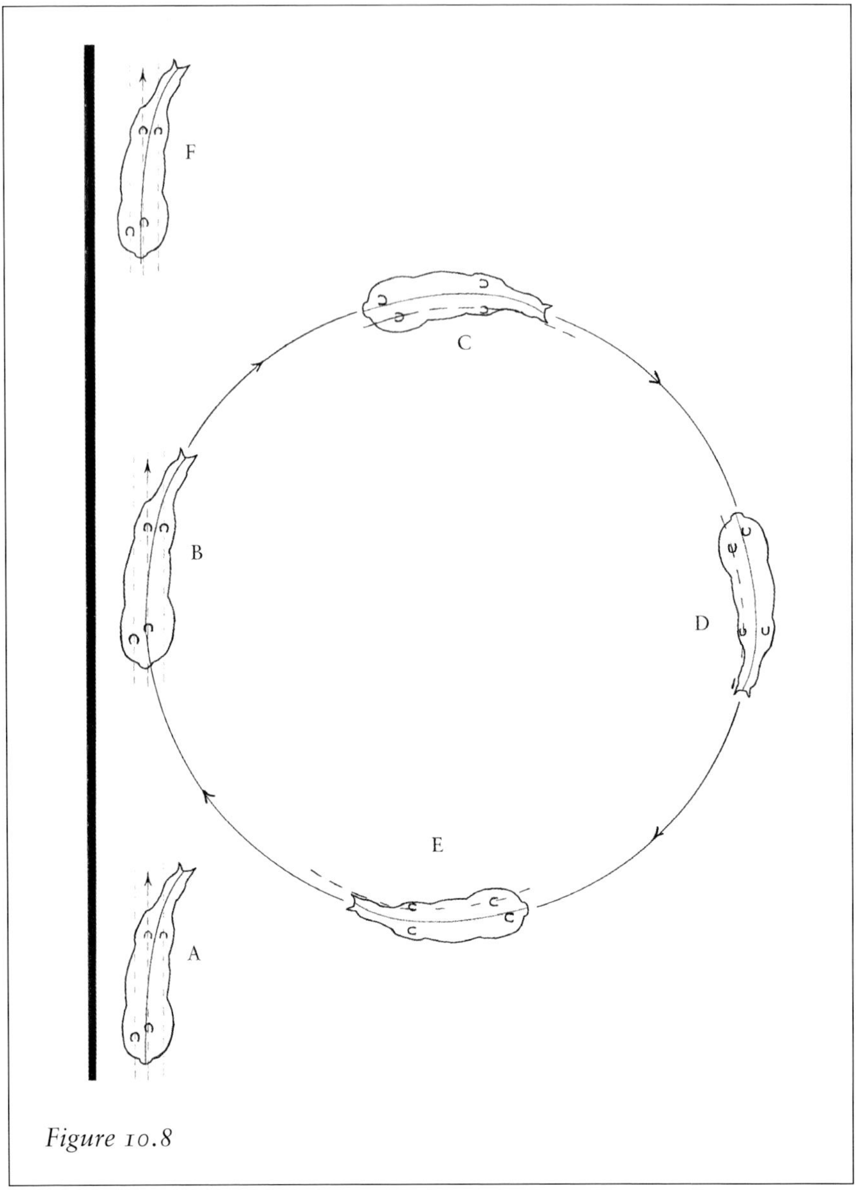

Figure 10.8 Shoulder-in to volte is an excellent exercise for both horse and rider. This diagram illustrates this as the shoulder-in is ridden along the wall of the arena A it can easily be converted at point B into a single-track circle with the horse's inside legs lined up (C, D, E). Furthermore, this demonstrates how, as the circle is completed, the shoulder-in can commence further along the wall once again from point B towards F. Because the bend in the horse should remain constant throughout this exercise, it underscores the importance of the rider's inside leg position remaining absolutely steady at the girth all the time.

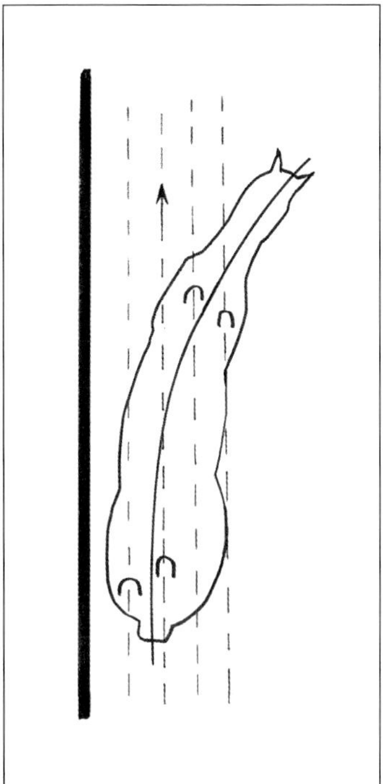

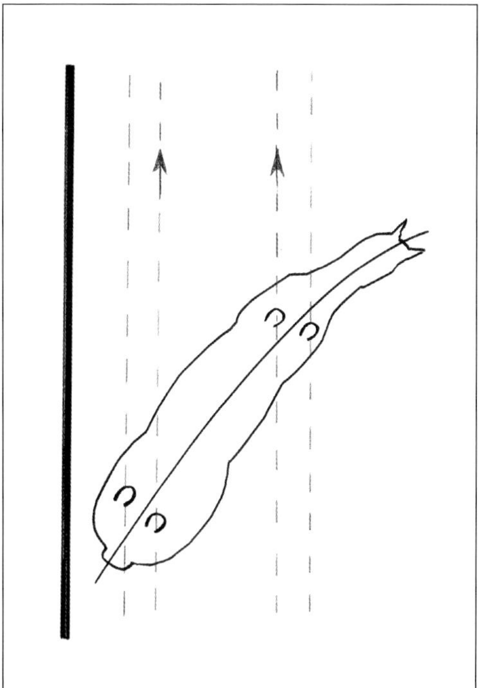

Figure 10.9 Four-track shoulder-in.

Figure 10.10 Leg-yielding away from rider's right leg at 45° angle to the wall. Shown here with the horse's nose facing into the arena.

STAGE VI

Travers or croup-in

10.39 – The croup is ridden more to the inside, either on three tracks (*Figure 10.11*), or on four tracks (*Figure 10.12*). Both are correct.

– This is the most advanced, **third phase, or type, of bending: bend and move *into* the bend.**

– It is a bending, suppling, collecting exercise.

– It is two-track work.

– The counter-exercise is **renvers.**

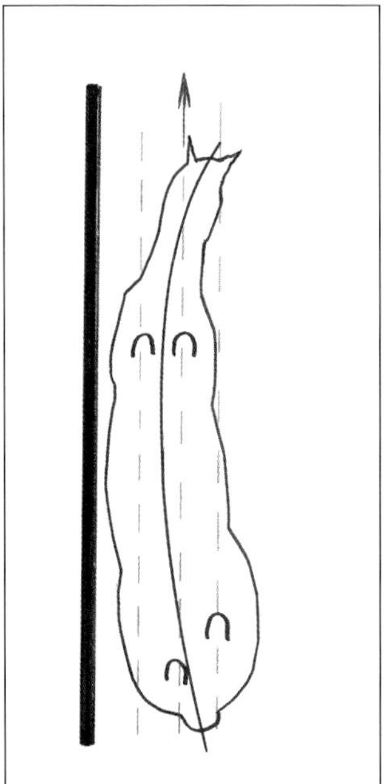

Figure 10.11

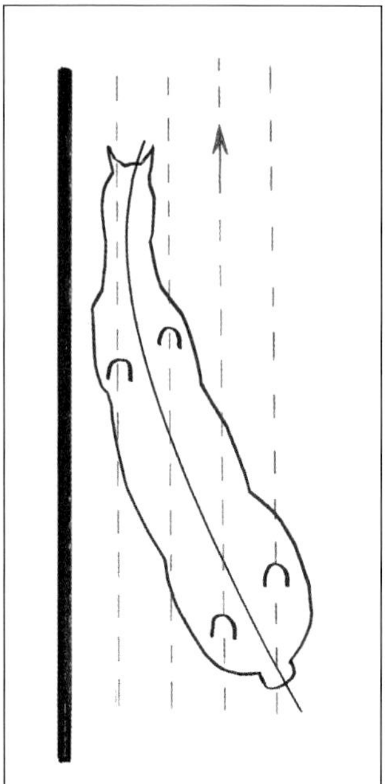

Figure 10.12

This position is the last to mature because, as a prerequisite to successful travers/croup-in work, the horse needs to be well seasoned in his understanding and responsiveness to the inside seat bone/leg (as a forward aiding influence; as a *passive* bending presence; and as a lateral yielding influence) and to have subsequently learned to understand and accept the outside aids (especially the outside rein). This can only be achieved through adequate preparation in the previous stages, in particular Stages II, IV and V. Thus, progressively:

a) single-track shoulder-fore (*Figure 10.2*);

b) two-track shoulder-fore (*Figure 10.6*); and finally,

c) the true shoulder-in (*Figure 10.7*)

These three are the foundation exercises for all two-track work. Travers (croup-in) is built on these.

10.40 The work must be considered seriously faulty when the outside leg/inside rein are the *predominant* aids to achieve either turns-on-the-haunches or the travers (half-pass, croup-in, or renvers) positions. On a continuous basis there must be a shoulder-in within the travers, and a travers within the shoulder-in. This means that the horse has properly learned to be soft to the rider's inside leg, and **with a forward intent** has learned to come up to – is received by and accepts – the outside aids. The shoulder-fore and shoulder-in are the best positions to learn to construct the desired inside-leg/ outside-rein oriented riding, which then naturally carries over into the correct travers/croup-in/half-pass position.

Note The terms 'travers' and 'half-pass' apply when Stage VI croup-in attitudes are ridden across the diagonal of the school, or from the centre line or quarter line back to the long-side wall of the arena.

10.41 A useful exercise to practise along the long wall of the school is going from shoulder-in, to single-track volte (*Figure 10.8*); then to croup-in, to single-track volte (*Figure 10.13*); then again shoulder-in, to single-track volte again, and then again croup-in, to single-track volte, back and forth. The exercise helps the rider to feel and understand how these two positions are interrelated and coordinated.

10.42 Through the appropriate use of travers, in judicious combination with the other positions described above, gradually and imperceptibly over the months and years the haunches grow in suppleness and in their ability to lower and carry more weight, until the ultimate manifestation of high degrees of collection are achieved. Even the deep levades, are possible without damaging the horse's joints and tendons. At this stage, transitions and turns-on-the-haunches are other useful training exercises to further polish, hone and balance our living work of art.

10.43 In concluding, it can not be sufficiently emphasized that two-track work is not an end in itself, but a temporary adjunct to training. Two-track work is only a form of exercising aimed at helping augment the malleability of the horse and thereby increasing the quality of the gaits in single-track work, where most of our riding and training should be carried out. The more advanced the rider is, and the further along the training of the horse has progressed,

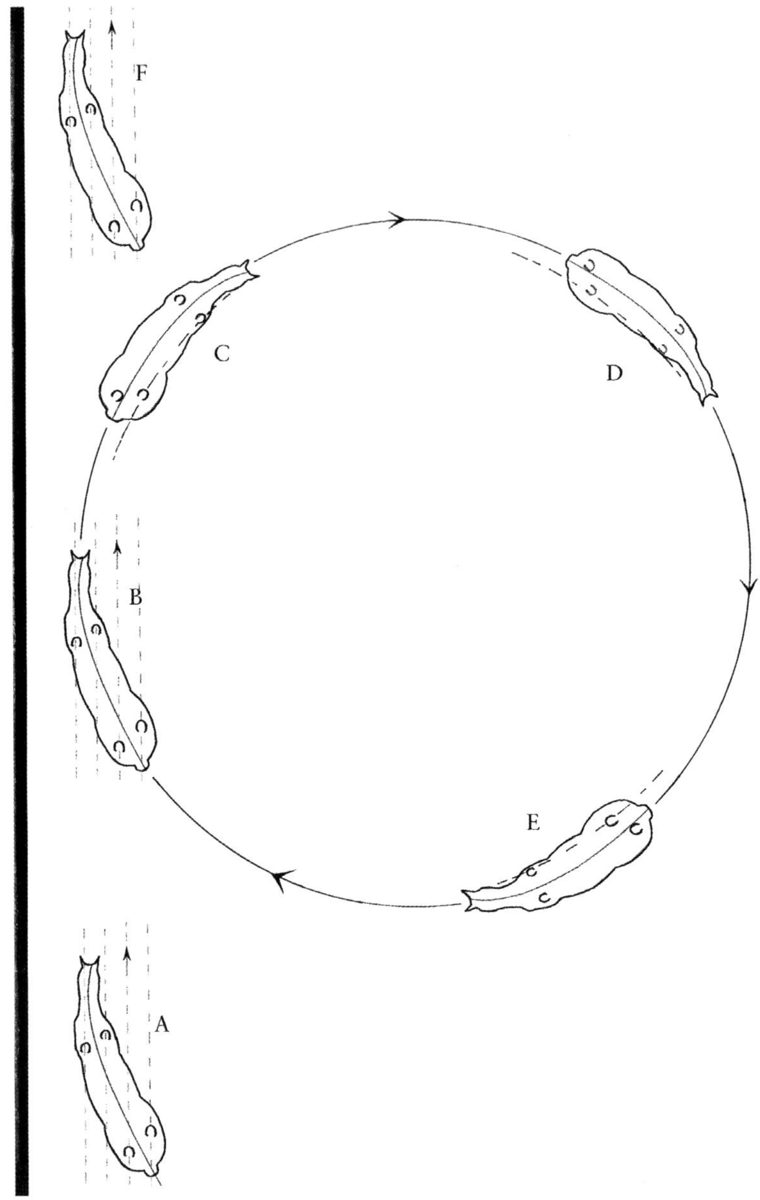

Figure 10.13

Figure 10.13. Croup-in to volte. This diagram shows how the croup-in at position A can easily be converted into a single-track volte at point B with the horse's inside legs lined-up around the circle (C, D, E); then to return again to croup-in along the wall again from B towards F.

the more the two-track exercises are used just very briefly, and often only microscopically, to refresh the alignment and balance of the horse as needed. These adjustments become ever more imperceptible to the observer. That is, after all, the true goal of fine riding: invisible interaction between the rider and horse!

B

CHAPTER XI

Ever Learning

The realization that he has always yet to learn brings the true rider to dedicate his life to this art.

RICHARD L. WÄTJEN

Introduction

11.0 Learning to ride is indeed a grand adventure. Besides the joy of interacting with the spirit of the horse, it is at the same time a journey through the landscape of our inner selves. When we are dedicated to seeking deeper understanding and harmony with the creature's truth, the interaction inevitably ends up stretching and fulfilling us in so many unforseen ways. This chapter broaches some of these less tangible, inner aspects, with the anticipation of helping to make the passage through the equestrian forest a little easier, more enjoyable and sure.

OPPOSITE PAGE

Above: *Margot Huelke on Gitano (¾ Andalusian, ¼ Arab cross, age 4–5 years.) Demonstrating an ideal working and training attitude for the young horse. The rider is in a fitting, independent, balanced, gentle position for the rising trot. Very fine work.*

Below: *Gitano, collected trot. Approximately 10 years later. A fortuitous comparison shot, capturing the same horse in the identical trot phase as above. Gitano has clearly developed beautifully in muscling and stature due to Margot's excellent, patient work. Here, the author riding during one of his clinics, demonstrating a not-so-perfect hand position (there is no technical advantage to having such a hand attitude). At this moment the rider has not as yet resolved independent balance in the horse. This is mirrored in the horse's tension against the left rein. When the rider is right, the horse will always be right.* Photo, Alston Wolf.

I ask the reader's forbearance if it appears that occasionally the obvious may have been stated. But it seems that plain things are at times easily overlooked. Such everyday matters have therefore also been included.

Part I · As Students

Seeking and finding ...

11.1 The old guideline 'Seek and ye shall find'[1] surely holds true for horsemanship. Attending lessons or clinics is but the first step. We must search tirelessly for the horse's truth on our own and leave no stone unturned. Only when we participate fully in the learning procedure – being wholly there, actively 'thinking with' the moments as they unfold can we be more readily helped by the horse and the teacher to gain understanding which leads to the joy of harmony we so desire.

Listen to it all

11.2 When in group lessons, it is best not to wait for comments or advice intended only for ourselves. Much can be gained if we let nothing slip our notice and do as though every word from the teacher (though ostensibly meant for someone else) is directed at us personally.

Making information ours

11.3 An essential part of learning is to experiment with the given information. We need to adopt the concepts and make them ours by adjusting them to the needs of the living moment on many different horses. It is also best to find a reasonable balance between time under instruction and time practising alone. Further, beware of the new-toy syndrome. That is, avoid latching onto that one

1 Matthew 7:7; Luke 11:9

new supertrick you learned yesterday, and end up forgetting all the other ancillary aspects which were underlying the success of that one good moment.

Impersonal road signs

11.4 We can make the most of our lessons when we take both criticism and accolades entirely impersonally. The more we remain emotionally unaffected by them, seeing them as nothing more than information or road signs to help us along the way, the more our understanding opens and the sooner we progress. The moment we allow ourselves to get hurt by taking things personally, valuable learning diminishes drastically.

It's the message

11.5 Though some teachers may be more reliable channels of truth than others, it is wise to follow truth rather than the messenger. In the end, we should rely on *the* source – the horse – not on opinions about, or reactions to, the source.

Ah, those good feelings

11.6 When mounting up the day after a good ride, it is easy to succumb to the temptation of immediately wanting to get back to those 'good feelings' from the day before. Yet, such attempts often fail because that bubble of joy we experienced in yesterday's ride caused us to neglect to take note of the step-by-step details which lead to that success. The remainder of the ride is thus spent in a cloud of frustration, aimlessly seeking those illusive feels. To quote the punch line of a joke, it is like '... looking in a dark room for a black cat, that isn't there!'[2] It is basically unhelpful

2 Two prelates, a Catholic and a Protestant, were having a theological fencing match, a real Donnybrook. After numerous impassioned forays, back and forth, out of sheer frustration the Catholic prelate finally blurted, 'You know what's the matter with you Protestants, you're looking in a dark room for a black cat, and you can't find it!' 'Oh, really!' retorted the Protestant, 'Well, you Catholics are looking in a dark room for a black cat, that isn't there!' [author unknown].

to chase after yesterday's good feels! This in no way suggests to ride without feeling! But, essentially, anyone knows when things feel better, even a rank beginner. However, to succeed we need to develop sufficient analytical powers and a sufficiently good memory to recognize and remember exactly how we arrived at those good moments. We must also have acquired enough experience and skill to reproduce the effective combinations consistently. That is, we need to acquire the ability to generate and maintain balanced freedom and carrying forwardness in the horse at any moment. There are three main ingredients for reproducing good feels, each one of equal importance.

1) To cultivate **good leadership** qualities: clarity of purpose and will applied (**4.11**).

2) To cultivate good, **positive attitudes**: we must be in control of our thoughts and emotions and have the right heart, mind and spirit towards the horse.

3) To be in command of good, **solid technicalities**.

These factors combined, will give those good feelings a greater chance of occurring more consistently.

Finding the way back

11.7 To produce consistently good results tomorrow, we need to become keenly aware and leave a trail of memory crumbs along the way today!

About roots

11.8 When we lose contact with the basics, our work loses significance. To quote the words of an ancient Master, 'Worldly people lose the roots and cling to the tree tops'.[3]

3 From *The Secret of the Golden Flower* translated by Richard Wilhelm, comments by C.G. Jung.

It's 'only' DNA!

11.9 Basic work is often dismissed as being easy, beginnerish stuff, below the worth of advanced riders. But to think in such terms would be like the construction crew of a great building discarding its foundations just because the roof was finally up. Truly, we love and honour the rose, but seem indifferent towards the stalk and roots; and even disdain the manure from which the coveted blossom springs. By its very nature, basic work can not help but fully engage any serious rider. If we earnestly seek beauty and harmony, we must respect the sacred laws which govern the horse. That is, we must learn to deal with the principle building blocks, the very DNA, of horsemanship. We must be constantly watchful to keep the foundation skills well honed and thoughtfully applied in all work.

The power of their words

11.10 It takes many years of steeping in a horse-harmonious, horse-centred environment, before the creatures' hidden truths gradually reveal themselves and before we can reliably begin to discern between good work and that which is not entirely so. An essential part of learning is to have correct theory at our fingertips by studying the literary works of past Masters.[4] It does not matter that it may take years to perfect the application of that theory, but at least our practice will be more meaningfully directed. It is also worthwhile to keep a detailed diary of our riding and to distil the notes down to a few brief points that can be easily memorized or quickly reviewed before mounting.

A happy balance

11.11 As with all things, the 'golden middle' is best. Without sufficient theory, practice is limited to the repertoire of a backyard hobby. When theory is overemphasized, our riding becomes too intellectual which suppresses the untroubled spontaneity so essential

4 See the Recommended Reading list.

to fine horsemanship. But, just as musicians need to play scales, so too riders initially need the structure of theory and imposed exercises and school figures to acquire technical skill and good habits. Then intuition and talent can gradually take over once again which allows natural flair to resurface in time.

Wright was right ...

11.12 'Skill comes by constant repetition of familiar feats rather than by a few overbold attempts at feats for which the performer is yet poorly prepared.' Wilbur Wright.

The periodic table

11.13 We need to have a thorough understanding of the essential nature of the raw material – the basic substance – with which we are working before we are able to cultivate or enhance it. For us riders that raw material or substance is the horse's nature.

The main **technical** indicators of correct, harmonious work are:

a) The purity of the basic gaits.

b) The horse's back is easy to sit on.

The main **psychological** indicators of honourable and ethical interaction with the horse are:

a) The creature remains mentally calm, confident, and content.

b) His personality and spirit ever prevail intact and remain cheerfully engaged.

More than I.Q.

11.14 Some things have to do with more than just technical know-how, physical dexterity, or I.Q. Training is one of those. It has to do with having intuitive feel for the horse, the measure of which is ineffable and unteachable. The good trainer is to the matter born.

About end users and programmers

11.15 To draw an analogy with the computer world: a person who can ride a trained horse is like an end user who knows how to click icons. Whereas a person who can train is like a programmer.[5] Nevertheless, there is good training (programming) – and not-so-good training (programming)! Here, an old computer acronym comes to mind, GIGO (garbage in, garbage out), i.e. reap what you sow. That surely applies to training horses!

Live what you know

11.16 Three steps to increased awareness and self-improvement are:

1) Through study **find out** what we need to do.

2) While practicing **think** of what we need to do, and **actually do that.**

3) Rather than waiting to be reminded by someone else, we must persistently, repeatedly, and continually **check on and remind ourselves** to make the necessary adjustments.

If we truly **live what we know** each moment of each day, we can trust implicitly that improvement will happen in due time.

Trial and error

11.17 Improvement develops through a process of trial and error. We need to act with confidence and have the freedom to experiment in the living laboratory of the horse to find out how to get things right. We must obviously avoid carelessness, such as being disrespectful towards the horse or repeatedly making the same errors. The Dutch have a humorous play on words about this common human shortcoming, it goes something like this: 'Is it **in-*stinct*** or intelligence? A donkey rarely bumps himself on the same rock twice, yet the human being appears to ***stink*-into it** [falls for it] each time again'.

5 Concept contributed by Susan Dummit.

They are *oh so loyal!*

11.18 Chocolates, chocolates, chocolates ... MMM-mmmmm ... we *do* love our old habits.

It brings us closer

11.19 Does practice make perfect? Not really. Only good, thoughtful practice brings us closer to perfection in time. Long hours of incorrect practice can only make us experts at doing things incorrectly. This leads us to the well-known quote on the definition of insanity, 'Doing the same thing over and over again and expecting different results!'[6]

Problems can become opportunities

11.20 Needless to say, at times we all make errors and find ourselves momentarily out of harmony. But through intelligent evaluation and effort at self-improvement, we can turn negatives into positives; problems become opportunities for learning and healing.

New contract ? OK!

11.21 Yesterday is dead and gone. We must not try to ride yesterday's horse. Ride *today's* horse! – and be *today's* rider! Bury the past in an unmarked grave. Retain only the positive aspects we have gained. It is not helpful to get bogged down in yesterday's shying or antics from the horse, or to be burdened by our own past mistakes. Instead, we must just 'keep on keeping on'[7] down the road and resolve to improve. After all, the best apology is simply to strive to do better next time. Horses are so wonderful! When we approach them with a good heart, we can write a new contract with them literally at any moment. We can make a fresh start, a new blank page on which to write better equestrian words each day. The creatures will virtually always play along with us (**2.20**). Here, a quote from an old hand at meeting life's challenges can

6 Author unknown.
7 Edgar Cayce.

help lighten our way, 'Success is going from failure to failure to failure – without losing your enthusiasm'. Winston Churchill.

Trouble is a-brewing

11.22 On the other hand, we sound a death knell to productive work the moment we look away from the simple requirement of our task – 'What can I do, here and now, on this day, to help *this* horse, with these symptoms, to go better?' – and begin instead to search for excuses as to why the horse is not going well. Truly, the moment we put *any* blame on the horse, however subtly, the lines are drawn, the battle begins and horsemanship leaves the scene. Though horses may indeed present us with all manner of difficulties, we can be liberated and give progress the best chance of occurring when we:

a) Stop confining ourselves and waste precious time and energy, by blaming circumstances or other people (whether they are actually to blame or not!).

b) Empower ourselves by seeking positive solutions to anything we encounter.

We must strive to become masters at what Edgar Cayce called, 'Turning stumbling blocks into stepping stones'.

OK; whose 'fault' is it anyway?

11.23 It is all really quite simple. If the horse goes poorly, it is the rider's fault. If the horse goes well, it is the rider's 'fault'. It follows then that we should praise the horse often, especially when we think he is *not* going very well. After all, *we* are the ones who have not yet helped him to go better!

Cluck, cluck, cluck

11.24 Riding is replete with chicken-and-egg situations. The rider is the chicken and the egg.

Talent galore, however

11.25 Regardless of the degree of youthful talent, there is no substitute for equestrian experience and maturity. To paraphrase Goethe, the finer qualities of horsemanship develop only once 'a little snow appears on the roof', that is, with the maturity, wisdom and experience that come with time, as does the greying of hair.

Remaining modest

11.26 It is easy to be humble when things are not going particularly well. In the 'inner game of riding', however, the challenge lies in remaining modest, especially as our talents start to blossom.

The accolade!

11.27 The most valuable ribbon, trophy, or equestrian certificate is the one awarded by the horse. It can either be presented or rescinded at any moment the rider occupies the saddle.

The pure performance

11.28 No reasonable person would want to deny anyone the joy of genuine accomplishment, nor of well-deserved recognition. But how much of our good energy is unreasonably siphoned off trying to gratify the desire for recognition? Isn't life rather about improving ourselves as individuals – becoming our own best – so that we may grow in a positive way and becoming joyful by enriching others with our talents and valid contributions? If our own best happens to be *the* best, that is admirable and worthy of recognition. Yet, isn't that purely incidental? Surely *the* competition, *the* performance is actually within – having mainly to do with ourselves? Thus the meaningful question is, 'Relative to the task at hand, how far have we developed ourselves compared to our own *actual* abilities and potential?' Surely the question is not, 'How do we rate in comparison to another person?' The first question is evaluated by the horse. The second question tends to be judged by humanity.

Shooting for what?

11.29 The Chinese sage Tranxu observed, 'When the archer shoots for no particular prize, he has all his skills. When he shoots to win a brass buckle, he is already nervous; when he shoots for a gold prize, he goes blind, sees two targets, and is out of his mind. His skill has not changed, but the prize divides him. He cares! He thinks more of winning than shooting, and the need to win drains him of his power.'[8]

Who will we serve?

11.30 The Good Book cautions: 'No man can serve two masters ...'[9]

True learning

11.31 Krishnamurti's words echo similar sentiments, 'True learning only begins once the competitive spirit has stopped'. At first, these words may seem absurd in our highly competitive society. Yet, when we look at the deeper meaning and purpose of our existence, they make absolute sense. Because honorable accomplishment comes only when the work is based on noble purpose and is in harmony with Natural Law – whether designing automobiles, aircraft, growing a garden, or learning to ride – and not when our main goal is merely to beat the competition. There certainly is room for healthy competition which can raise the standard of products or individual performance. But, as with all things, competition can be worthy or unworthy. We need only think of hostile takeovers of companies to see the darker side of this subject, when human greed and egotism begin to rule. Whether we are competing or not, if striving for truth and excellence is our master, our accomplishments are worthy, our lives are honourable, and horses are ennobled through our interaction with them. However, if our main goal is only to beat the competition and win a ribbon, we are – in the moral sense – on a very slippery

8 Anthony de Mello's *Awareness: The Way to Love.* The quote contributed by Jane Skiba.
9 Matthew 6:24

slope. If we are not careful, it is on just that slope that so many good horses are unfairly subjugated, being sacrificed on the altar of our unruly, self-serving ego. On just this subject, there was an uplifting interview on Frank Elstner's TV programme *People of the Week*, in which respected German news anchor woman Judith Rakers was asked about her passion for riding. Among other things, she shared this personal reflection with the viewers, 'There came a point in my riding in which I felt I had to make a decision. I asked myself if my horse was my friend or a sports apparatus. I decided he was my friend.'

Holier than thou

11.32 Whether partaking in competitions, or following classical riding for its own sake without competing, neither is better or worse. Worthy is worthy, and unworthy is unworthy. After all, it is not so much *what*, but *how* we achieve what we do that counts. The riding task is altogether too huge for any one of us to be smug or self-satisfied, or to start pointing fingers and being overcritical or demeaning of others. Horsemanship requires of us sound character and absolute integrity – engaging all that is good, worthy and honourable in us. We need to grow through the experiences in daily riding towards an ever-better level of self-mastery, especially the quality of our heart's desire and the merit of our thoughts. That is, we need above all to learn to ride and control our 'inner horse'. The better we are at that, the sooner our 'outer horse' will, like magic, become easier and more enjoyable to work with.

Cream rises

11.33 Cream rises! It's the Law! If we remain true to our ideal, excellence invariably comes to the top, though it may take many years of persistent struggle to develop that in ourselves and in our work. And it may take yet more years for its truth to be recognized, appreciated and acknowledged by the world out there. Truly, there is no contribution too small or too lowly. What counts is that we do our own best! It does not matter whether our input is seen by others, or hidden behind the scene as part of the fundamental workings of another person's or establishment's accomplishments. Honest, well-grounded work can not help but become part of the timeless treasures of humanity, irrespective of culture, race or creed. We need only think of the lives of great painters, composers and scientists who suffered disdain and impoverishment during their lives because of the envy, backbiting, narrow-mindedness or the unknowingness of the people at the time. Yet, these giants of humanity became immortalized because they stuck with their principles. Their profound contribution was validated in time through the undeniable power, beauty and truth of their art and science.

Establishing personal ideals

11.34 The following points, I believe, are surely worthy of consideration as we set our personal equestrian ideals:

a) Striving ever to improve ourselves to become our own best.

b) Studying to gain an ever-deeper understanding of the horses, to live in ever-greater harmony with them.

c) Serving horses by taking the best possible care of them while they are in our stewardship.

d) Being fair and reasonable in the requests we make from the horse while riding.

e) Being ever grateful for having the privilege of being in the horse's presence; and for their generosity of allowing us to sit on and interact with them.

Part II · As Teachers

Establishing teaching ideals

11.35 Besides aspiring to the above standards, the following are high on my personal list of teaching ideals.

a) To foster respect for horses, to be an emissary for them, a loyal guardian of their needs.

b) To be respectful of the pupil, to champion sound values and inspire excellence.

c) To be a mediator between horse and rider, so that harmony can ensue through mutual understanding.

d) To make myself obsolete as soon as possible by advocating independence; encouraging students to cultivate the ability to learn directly from the horse, while developing trust in their own abilities.

e) To have as my sole motivation for all guidance the fulfilling of the specific needs of the horse or rider at any given moment.

f) To practise what I preach to the very best of my ability. Avoid the, 'Do as I say – not as I do', scenario.

What motivates?

11.36 Surely, our riding, training and teaching become impoverished if we let the superficiality of some arbitrary schedule of external events, such as an impending competition or the age of a horse, rule the rate of training.

It's in the doing

11.37 Good example is by far the most incisive message.

Dialogue

11.38 A teacher may know exactly what is needed and be able to explain their intention efficiently and eloquently. Yet, it is surprising how something so perfectly clear can be so entirely misunderstood! It is therefore helpful for both teacher and pupil to encourage dialogue. It enriches the learning/teaching environment for both.

In the same boat

11.39 How can we as teachers possibly propagate the highest degree of equestrian truth, unless we are prepared to acknowledge the occasional deficiencies in our own riding, rather than trying to justify them? Then again, it is equally important for the student to accept, even appreciate, that every teacher has strengths and weaknesses, and to recognize that both aspects can be instructive simply by striving to emulate the good while avoiding those particular imperfections that challenge the teacher. In the end, isn't it the overall respect, quality and decency of the interaction between the teacher, the pupil and the horse, that counts most? Surely that is the hallmark of a healthy, constructive learning environment.

Part III · Choosing Suitable Teachers or Stables

11.40 It is both enriching and wonderful that there are many different teachers, approaches, and riding disciplines to choose from. Therefore, besides deciding on the type of riding and the tenor of the surroundings to which a heart may be inclined, each individual needs to find a trainer or instructor with whom they feel comfortable.

To be able to make a reasonable and fair assessment of a teacher's way of working, auditing their clinics is time well spent. It provides one the opportunity to observe the person working with different horses and pupils for at least several days.

In commencing this search, however, it is essential to acknowledge that any one, even the best among us, occasionally have clay feet. And since examples of living perfection are rare indeed, it would not be beneficial to be overly critical. At the very same time, it would also not be wise to put discernment aside and turn a blind eye to that which might be considered genuinely unacceptable behaviour.

The most essential part of making our choices is to keep foremost in mind that riding has to do with the nature of the horse, and striving to grow ever more harmonious with that nature. Therefore, those teachers and facilities that clearly put the horses' wellbeing first, by treating them kindly and respectfully, should be given priority when considering prospects for one's equestrian education.

A watercolour portrait of Riffa, *Kladruber school horse at Reitinstitut Egon von Neindorff Foundation. Monika Bartsch. 2009. 30 x 40 cm.*

CHAPTER XII

The Hidden Face of Horsemanship

Nature is the only book which offers profound content on each leaf.
WOLFGANG GOETHE

12.1 Why does riding so grip us and entice us ever onward in search of the spirit of the horse? Surely there must be something more there below the surface, other than the palpable pleasure of riding and being uplifted by these lovely creatures. To discover just what that 'something' might be, let us for a moment go beyond the commonplace aspects of riding and explore the fascinating hidden dimensions of this subject. This venture inevitably takes us into the more ethereal aspects of our human make-up. Here we can begin to see just how deeply the intangible elements of our existence influence the activity of riding; and conversely, how horsemanship intimately affects every aspect of our lives. To begin, let us see what the ancients have to tell us about life and our place in it. Why are we here?

What the ancients have to tell us

12.2 From a broad spectrum of human philosophy spanning many cultures and vast stretches of time, the ancients tell us that life on this earth in a physical body, bound by time and space, is a most special opportunity. They explain that life is an avenue for personal growth which allows us to experience first hand the universal laws of cause and effect. Through these immutable laws the consequences of our decisions – our thoughts, words and actions – are faithfully reflected in our environment, in our fellow man, and in the creatures we contact. If we care to listen to them, these archetypal precepts can guide us to make ever-better choices which, in turn, give us an ever-greater sense of purpose, fulfillment and joy in our days.

Our human make-up

12.3 To gain a deeper insight into how these universal principles influence us, let us take a closer look at the function of each aspect of our human make-up – body, mind and spirit. The spirit is the life force, the very essence, the movement of our being. How this spirit force is used is determined solely by us exercising our individual birthright – the power of free will. Every decision we make is ours to choose just as we wish, positively or negatively. The mind, on the other hand, is the creative builder. It is the generator of ideas with which we can set our ideals and construct ways of accomplishing our purposes and desires. The mind is also a vehicle of discernment which governs our will and enables us to analyze our performance relative to the ideals and objectives we have set. Everything must come into existence in the unseen world of the mind and spirit – the realm of creative planning – before it can be brought into manifestation through the act of physical effort. That is where the body finally comes into the picture, as the instrument through which we are able to express ourselves and bring our thoughts, desires and purposes into visible, tangible reality.

Horsemanship's special role

12.4 If these elements are constantly in play in all human activity, why would horsemanship be so distinctly well suited to help in our personal development?

By embracing the challenges of horsemanship, we become increasingly aware of who and what we are, and how our decisions and actions affect the world around us. This is so because in riding we are called upon to attain exceptionally refined degrees of control, not only over the mind, spirit and emotions, which inescapably flavour the tone of our message to the horse, but we must gain superb command over our body. There is more involved, however, than just achieving dynamic harmony with the horse's movement. The body must at the very same time incorporate the **guiding message** within its presence – delivering its 'wordless words' through the physical senses to our equine dancing partners.

Those marvellous mirrors!

12.5 This distinct requirement challenges us in every aspect of our being, and simultaneously gives us the opportunity to experience the level of self-mastery we have attained, as it is spontaneously reflected in the living mirror of the horse. What a blessing these pure, untainted mirrors are to us! Whether king or pauper, horses accept us as we are, and echo with exquisite impartiality and benign candidness the state of those three major elements of our make-up: body, mind and spirit.

A revelation

12.6 Taking us yet further into the hidden realms of horsemanship, we can experience through the horse the remarkable truth that *thoughts are things*. Indeed, the creatures reveal to us, because of their uncanny sensitivity, that not only physical actions or spoken words, but every emotion, every feeling, every attitude, every desire, every concept *we merely think*, regardless of its subtlety, has indeed got a definite influence or repercussion in the world around us. In other words, the laws of cause and effect apply just as much to the mental and spiritual realm as they do the physical. Without distinction, these very same precepts seamlessly interpenetrate both worlds. Horsemanship therefore can be instrumental in helping us become aware of the importance of learning to control our minds – to understand and respect the power of thinking – and leads us to weigh each thought ever more guardedly.

Where the buck stops

12.7 An essential aspect to success is that we choose to look honestly at the reflection horses show us and resolve not to blame the creatures for any difficulties we may encounter. Rather, irrespective of the trials, we must seek solutions exclusively in ourselves. All our interactions must be entirely free of criticism, reproach, resentment and vengeance. Only through exercising benign leadership – that is, providing the indispensable element of purpose to the work, and dedicating ourselves to serving the horse's needs faithfully – are we able to unlock the creature's natural generosity and talents. This helps us transcend difficulties more easily and virtually dispenses with the need for 'obedience'.

A solemn appreciation

12.8 What a glorious moment it is when we come to realize that horses have taught us a great deal more than we have taught them. That, on our way to better understanding, through the long and trying days of our unknowingness, the creatures have gone through many of our inner challenges and crises with us and have endured it all with saintly patience. In facing and accepting this truth, a nameless mixture of emotions wells up inside – feelings of gratitude, reverence and love towards our four-legged friends – knowing just how much we have been enriched through our interaction with them.

Why do we ride?

12.9 In reflecting on the words of the ancients, that our lives are meant to be a school for our soul, it becomes ever more clear how, if we are willing to listen to the gentle spirit of the horse – in all its simple beauty – we can be kindly and patiently assisted in fulfilling that essential purpose for our existence on this good earth. Such is the embodiment of this our passion – the deeply personal art of riding.

The Appaloosa. *Monika Bartsch. Oil on canvass, 2001. 50 x 60 cm.*

CHAPTER XIII

On Stewardship

13.1 As we have seen in the previous chapter, abstract concepts play a vital part in helping us better understand our role in the equestrian task and enable us to enjoy more fully our relationship with the horse. High on the list of priorities of such ethereal topics is the concept of stewardship.

13.2 Why is stewardship so important, and how does it pertain to our interaction with the horse? Let us take a moment to explore some of the basic aspects of this subject more thoroughly.

What is stewardship?

13.3 The dictionary[1] defines a steward as, 'One who serves by managing the financial affairs or property of another; or who administrates anything as the agent of another or others'.

13.4 In this definition, several impressions command our attention. One of them is, 'serves'. In other words, if we are to be considered good stewards, willing service is surely indispensable. Another noteworthy point is, 'property of *another*'. This implies responsibility. It confirms for us that, despite the broad freedom and power a steward might be given, such a person always remains accountable to their employer or master: the property owner.

1 *Merriam Webster's Collegiate Dictionary*, Tenth Edition.

Who owns what?

13.5 Here, a clarification goes begging as to exactly who owns what. First, over which things have we been given only stewardship, for which we are fully accountable to our Master? And second, over which things do we have freedom to deal with as we wish? What can we actually consider 'ours'?

13.6 In reflecting on this, I believe we can not help but conclude that – even though we can technically possess belongings of every kind – we are actually no more than stewards over all material things in our lives. We own virtually nothing. We are given things for our temporary use only, after which they are no longer at our disposal, either due to circumstances in life, or death itself. Even with something as apparently permanent as real estate or property, the deed we hold could be seen as nothing more than a lifetime lease.

Charge over living aspects

13.7 Taking this concept a step further, not only are we temporary administrators of inanimate things in our lives, we are also guardians of the living aspects of existence: the earth's environment, vegetation, or the creatures in our care, not to mention our children or dependants. And finally, the least obvious though possibly among the most important to consider, we are also no more than stewards of the life energy we are given – any of our physical or spiritual powers and talents are only on loan, ours to use wisely or unwisely.

Free will

13.8 If we do not even own our life energy and talents, what can we possibly call ours?

As I perceive it, we own our individuality (consciousness of being) and our free will, and that which we build within ourselves, positively or negatively, by exercising that free will. In other words, by the power of free will we impel the desires of our hearts into action; and by using the mind (the generator of ideas) as the cognitive instrument to create ways of achieving our desire, we either intelligently, lovingly and wisely administrate – or selfishly, foolishly, or ignorantly squander – the life energy and talents we have been given. So, basically speaking, through the many large and small choices we make each day, we gradually form and come to 'own' that which we make of ourselves. We become that which we have thought, desired and done.

All in our own hands

13.9 Appropriately, by the power of our free will we are agents of our own destiny. Because, irrespective of the favourable or adverse circumstances in which we find ourselves, we are (within the limits of our awareness, talents and abilities) responsible for our thoughts, words, and subsequently, the deeds or physical manifestations which result from them. We horsemen, therefore, are responsible for our relationship with horses as well as for their wellbeing while they are in our care. Accordingly, it is our foremost duty to come to know enough about these creatures that, to the best of our ability, we do not in any way cause them mental or physical grief, either because of ignorance about their nature, or due to lack of control over ourselves while we are dealing with them.

Dedication …

13.10 Assuming full responsibility for our role as 'Steward' – that is, knowing we do not really ever own horses, but are merely their temporary guardians – is, without a doubt, one of the most important details of our equestrian activities. It deeply affects everything we do, and brings us to live by the central creed of this office: to dedicate ourselves to serving horses' needs faithfully, like a good gardener who does not think it lowly to be a servant to the seedlings, plants and trees in their care.

Attitude

13.11 Through our basic outlook, horses can sense from our 'vibrations' *how* we think. This applies not only to each aid but, more importantly, it affects the sum total of our entire riding and training schema. Our attitude imparts to horses whether or not we sincerely love them, are doing our best to understand them, and are genuinely concerned about their welfare. The horses will invariably respond accordingly. Such is the nature of fine riding, and through it we come to own that part of ourselves which has been formed and enriched through encounters with these most lovely of creatures.

Central role and purpose

13.12 When seen in this light, the horse's role is one of contributing partner, not dull-witted slave. Man's role as steward, is one of intelligent, trustworthy, benevolent leadership; one which proffers to the horse all the consideration, respect and honour he is due as a fellow member of God's creation. In this way we meet the noble horse not to exploit him for our own selfish ends, but instead, by invoking the finer qualities of our human nature, we fulfil the central purpose of our stewardship: to cultivate, nourish and enhance all things and creatures and souls over which we have been given charge. With this understanding as our prime motivation, we are able to join together harmoniously with our equine partners to create beautiful and above all mutually enjoyable, living works of art.

The author riding Lipizzaner stallion Thais, working trot left, at the Reitinstitut Egon von Neindorff. Good technicalities are shown with the poll at the highest point and the horse's face in front of the vertical. The rider's posture is vertical and the hand is on the line drawn from the bit to the elbow. Though this shows pleasant, harmonious work and a contented horse, a bit more energy and freedom would improve this moment. Photo, E. Richter.

CHAPTER XIV

Our Equestrian Family

After the game the King and Pawn go in the same box.

Italian proverb

14.1 In this chapter another outlook on riding will be explored which involves our 'greater equestrian family'. When seen from a broader perspective, whether we are masters of the art of riding or beginners, the subject of horsemanship is far greater than any one of its participants. It is a collective endeavour. It will therefore require our combined human effort to continue to uphold and apply the invaluable information – the truths about the horse's nature – gleaned over the centuries at great human effort and at the patient forbearance of so many dear horses. Towards this end, whether we are aware of it or not, it is important for us to accept that each and every one of us does influence this shared world of riding. And, if we accept our individual role in this larger picture, we can become part of a renaissance towards cultivating excellence in horsemanship in our time.

Let us see how we can best partake in this inspiring, worthy endeavour.

Like the cells of a body

14.2 Like the cells of a physical body, we are all members of the greater family of horsemanship. Not withstanding that some cells and organs are perhaps more significant than others, unless each cell does its part well the entire body suffers. This applies whether we are in a high profile position in the horse world, or working off on our own somewhere in the back woods. Inevitably, we all influence this equestrian community to a greater or lesser degree, either positively or negatively, by the way we ride, train and teach; and by how we generally interact with our horses. Accordingly, it is surely of pressing importance that we each take to heart our obligation towards all other 'apples' in the equestrian barrel, if we are to assure good health and positive growth for the entire community.

Our contribution

14.3 How can we make the most constructive contribution?

It is not usually the lack of quality horses, nor time, nor the lack of equestrian talent that is the greatest challenge in raising the quality of horsemanship in general. Rather, because overall advancement in riding is surely inseparable from the quality of each individual's personal attributes, I believe the answer to raising the general quality of horsemanship lies in one of Mahatma Gandhi's well-known adages, 'If you want to change the world, start with yourself'. Heaven only knows just how difficult that can be, but let's be daring and take a stab at doing just that – changing and improving ourselves for the sake of others and, of course, for the sake of the dear horses!

Establishing worthwhile goals

14.4 To direct our efforts usefully, it is essential that we begin by setting clear, worthwhile goals or ideals, on a personal as well as an equestrian front (**2.8**). In the absence of well-directed aspirations, all the knowledge, physical ability and talent in the world, however necessary or important they may be, will not produce entirely worthwhile results. It would be like having knowledge without wisdom, or love without a recipient. For example, just wanting to ride at Grand Prix level is not really a very helpful goal as such. However, wanting to grow in deeper understanding of the horse, and learning to work in closest harmony with his nature, that surely is an entirely worthwhile goal. By mastering that, high quality Grand Prix exercises will develop in due time as a logical consequence. We can approach our goal more reliably with honesty and integrity by patiently dedicating ourselves to a worthy purpose – one step at a time – in everyday practice. Then everything so deeply hoped for will follow as a natural outcome of such well-directed, personal effort.

A measure of self

14.5 We can best measure our progress by letting those unfailing laws of cause and effect be our guide to self-improvement. Because it is exactly through these laws that life, with unerring accuracy, presents us with precisely those circumstances which not only display and encourage our finer talents, but also reveals to us those areas that still need work. That, however, is neither a coincidence nor is it cruel. It is all really very hopeful and a blessing in disguise; not only if it initiates self-examination but when it awakens the desire to take corrective action, we are well on the road to improvement and healing. Inasmuch as only those corrections we make in ourselves, through our own will and persistent effort, can have lasting and worthwhile effects and bring the real growth we were meant to undergo.

Our personal choice

14.6 Clearly, it is up to us. Through exercising our free will we can choose to be in harmony and take responsibility for the sake of our own growth, which in turn contributes positively to the greater good. Or we can elect to be a source of imbalance, friction, or divisiveness in the world around us. Here, with stubborn determination, we choose to go our own way, feathering our own nest and lording over others or the horses at their expense. At first this may seem like a good idea. Yet, exploitation of any kind is a violation of Nature. And Nature will, sooner or later, with unmitigated clarity revolt against infractions of its laws in order to rebalance itself.

Who is to blame?

14.7 So often we seem not to recognize that much of the pain and disharmony we experience is that finger of the law pointing at us, saying, 'You are going wrong. Amend your ways!' But instead of listening, we end up evading the learning opportunity by projecting our misery onto the horse or other people, or by blaming it on fate or circumstances. Surely it is someone or something else's fault, never ours. But, actually, exactly the opposite is true in most cases and we simply must learn to accept our portion of the blame and strive to rectify our ways. How dearly essential it is that we do not waste precious time with costly evasions. For if we do, we will not only have cheated ourselves of the vital opportunity to advance and become more beautiful souls, but we will also have short-changed our fellow man by denying the world of the richness of our own unique creative capacity. It is through just this creative capacity we are meant to give joy to all those we meet, and through which we could give thanks, honour and praise to our Creator.

Overcoming

14.8 It is admittedly a demanding task to correct ourselves, because our personal obstacles are so close to the nerve, the very essence of our being. Our egos and self-worth are inextricably involved. When we do decide to take on the task of improving, however, we need to be patient and give ourselves time to outgrow poor habits with steady, enduring effort rather than a burst of short-term zeal. The best results come when we gradually replace unwanted traits with better, more wholesome tendencies until these improvements have themselves become habitual. In this way the negative aspects simply wither away through disuse because we no longer lend them any of our life energy. Through carefully avoiding all forms of negativity and concentrating instead on patiently developing good attitudes and a joyful spirit, we can make the best of most circumstances. In this way we become ever more adept at mastering the ever-unpredictable dance of life and of riding.

Interdependence

14.9 This wonderful venture we call riding is, in the deepest sense, wholly symbiotic. It is an inseparable interrelationship which applies not only between each horse and rider individually, but also just as much between all riders and horses in the equestrian community. Therefore it is surely worthwhile to keep in mind, and allow ourselves to be guided by, that basic universal truth – the clear, unambiguous language of cause and effect. Positive feeds off positive and grows towards joy and harmony. Negative feeds off negative and snowballs into ever unhappier, more difficult situations. We reap what we sow. Which will we choose?

Our commitment to each other

14.10 Let us then strive to engage our finest human qualities and be committed to support and assist each other by being gentle, kind, patient, tolerant, helpful and understanding in our mutual struggles to create finer levels of horsemanship. Through such choices we can become ever-better contributing members of our equestrian family and fulfil our part in the Great Design. This commitment inevitably expands its benevolent rays into the secret avenues of our soul and leads to genuine fulfilment and lasting happiness in all we do.

That which is Divine is, simply – Divine!

Barrel-spiral galaxy NG4314. Image courtesy of The Hubble Heritage Team (STScI/AURA) and NASA.

CHAPTER XV

On Nature

15.1 What is 'Nature'?

Einstein expressed his view about the resplendence of Nature with one of his characteristically thought-provoking descriptions: 'Nature does not hide her secrets by way of ruse, but because she is so essentially lofty'.

15.2 Indeed, isn't it exactly because the underpinnings from which manifest Nature springs are so deeply secreted from our everyday perceptions that, in some indefinable place of our being, a gnawing desire to gain deeper understanding seems always to linger? Yet, ironically, as we become ripe to comprehend them, little by little, the mysteries of Nature reveal themselves to us with apparent nonchalance, reposing as they do in the awesome power of their truth.

15.3 It is not really surprising then, that we are given some unexpectedly generous hints, right there in our daily comings and goings, which provide an opportune glimpse into Nature's secrets. These become evident if, for example, we take note of the difference between a dead stick lying on the forest floor and a living branch. Though both have the same substance, one is a viable manifestation, the other a discarded vessel, empty of its spirit purpose, relegated to being recycled through Nature's clearing house.

15.4 Surely a remarkable truth is revealed in this basic difference – especially that which rests in the quiet eloquence of the living branch. Through this example I sense the causative power of this vibrant cosmos as being entirely volatile. It is the very epitome of flexibility which follows principle rather than stagnant structure and pursues but one, single calling – to manifest *Life* – and in so doing reflects and honours its Creator – the Life, the Light, the Love and the Law of the universe. It is the work of Divine will, Divine purpose, emanating from the exquisite mind – the compelling thought force of pure Cosmic Consciousness. It is embodied *desire* crystalized into the astounding variety and beauty of tangible matter.

15.5 An insightful adage states, 'Success is a prepared force meeting an opportunity'. That is surely the ultimate interpretation of Nature's domain: an entirely fluid, malleable realm; a plasma of charged potential – walled-up Life Force – straining at the leash to burst onto the scene; adapting endlessly, mutating uninhibitedly in order to do so. It is constantly interdependent, interactive, symbiotic, irrepressible – like vegetation burgeoning forth from barren volcanic ash, or pressing up through cracks in stone or concrete – fueled by that relentless, living, breathing creative desire, ever prepared to manifest physically through an eternal stream of cycling.

15.6 When viewed in this light, all outward phenomena of Nature could be seen as a slow river, always appearing the same yet always new. It is only able to manifest through a process which constantly replenishes its elements – just as any one life is constantly being *re*-represented by new cells which ceaselessly and imperceptibly replace the old. The only thing that is unchanging is the living will, the living law, the living purpose within each atom, each cell, each body which draws to itself the desired matter needed to manifest tangibly through that process of cycling. Some embodiments cycle with astonishing speed (rudimentary life forms). Others, such as stars and galaxies, take immense eons to complete the sure-footed Word of their intended destiny – breathing in … breathing out … breathing in … breathing out …

15.7 The river of horsemanship is surely no exception. It runs on the invisible desire-fuel, emanating from the creative will of the rider. The fleeting equestrian dance can only be viably manifested and maintained when riders provide it with a continual replenishment of 'horse-harmonious *cells* of action' in their daily riding and handling. And on a larger scale, the magnificent river of equestrian art can only be perpetuated over the years through the steady flow of new young horses and new dedicated, modest, unpretentious riders – those who desire to carry the baton of equestrian truth in their own work and strive to pass it on to the next generation.

15.8 In light of this, it is clear that the greater our individual desire and skill to be suitably adaptive to the needs of the moment – being volatile, dynamic and lawful – the greater the chances are of us finding harmony with the ever-fluid motion of life as it is written in the horse. And thus, through developing good habits, we spontaneously, and ever more automatically, begin to nourish, to honourable advantage, the seed of the moment about to come – punctuated with countless little cycles of aiding to adjust the horse; or of corrections to ourselves towards our intended purpose – whereby the performance opportunely transforms into a radiant embodiment of seamless beauty.

15.9 Our interaction with the horse is validated when the creature flourishes and thrives under our care: becomes ever more beautiful, more vibrant, more joyful, more glorious, more free, more expressive, more ebullient. But the joy of harmony entirely eludes us the moment we try to forge external symptoms by artifice. Or, should we perchance stumble upon harmony, that we then try to hold the lovely moment still, trying to keep it to ourselves – plucking it off the conveyer belt of life, so to speak. For then we also come away empty handed. For horsemanship can only manifest through us by us hurling ourselves into it as tenable, vibrant members of its living truth. Otherwise we become no more than an impediment – a dead stick – obstructing just that which we most desire: the beauty of the horse's natural ability to move himself, based on us nurturing the blossom of his willing participation.

15.10 Let us then strive to put self aside and work in harmony with Natural Law, stamped as it is upon our very soul – with conscience as its utterance – and so keep ourselves always as a living branch on the Living Tree of Life: that all-encompassing Power and Majesty and Truth manifesting with infinite variety in that which we call Nature.

Liselott Linsenhoff, consummate winner of multiple dressage championships in Europe, the world, and at the Olympic games. Here she is riding thoroughbred horse Monarchist at the medium trot. An exquisitely lovely moment. The epitome of gracefulness, balance and harmony. Note the synchronized diagonal movement and the bend in the knee and hock, indicating the horse's back is correctly engaged.

CHAPTER XVI

Thoughts for 'On the Way'

If you seek truth you will not seek victory by dishonourable means, and if you find truth you will become invincible.

EPICTETUS

16.1 It is surely the province of but an elite few superbly talented individuals to free-climb sheer rock faces, in the equestrian sense. Most riders need to take somewhat surer, more well-demarcated paths to the summit, appreciating that the journey to fine horsemanship is a process, a gradual development of individuality, moral character and physical skill, not to mention gaining the broadest possible comprehension and mastery of equestrian principles based on the inexhaustible wisdom of Nature. If we seem not to have the patience or the desire to deal with the process, we have surely somewhat misjudged the size of the task that classical riding sets before us.

16.2 In order to approach our equestrian ideal with any degree of surety, we need to remain ever close to the serene depths of our heart to hear the subtle, yet laser-like guidance from the inner circle where truth abides. For unless we do, we can so readily become disconnected from this wellhead of vital nourishment by the loudness of the day crowding in against our soul, robbing it of its vitality and sacred purpose. Only through the integrity of untroubled patience can we settle down to accept the process which leads to excellence, instead of being constantly vexed by the journey, like small children in a car who keep wailing, 'Are we there yet?'

16.3 In the absence of such understanding, we inevitably fall into the trap of taking shortcuts, which beckon enticingly away from the main road, but seldom lead to harmonious interaction with the horse. We can become so mesmerized by our ambition to attain some arbitrary level of achievement that, in our glazed, myopic stare, we dismiss the living truth only to embrace emptiness – an equestrian moth, spellbound by the dancing flame of unmerited acquisition.

16.4 Let us then resolve to devote ourselves to a higher calling and make it our most passionate quest to climb the true equestrian mountain so that we may, through our travail in the saddle, become a living torch to the ideal, and bring the singular beauty of indissoluble communion with the horse into manifestation, each day again, as well as we possibly can; that those with seeing eyes and feeling hearts may be inspired to greater purposefulness and joy in their own riding, and in their lives.

We are but temporary stewards over the horse.
If we are to have equestrian integrity, we must faithfully conform to the creature's nature; all else is unfair and unworthy of the horse and diminishes our humanity.
The horses will ever remain our pure and ultimate judges; let us always listen to them.

13. *Enter by the narrow gate: for wide is the gate and broad is the way that leads to destruction, and there are many who go in by it.*

14. *Because narrow is the gate and difficult is the way which leads to life, and there are few who find it.*

Matthew 7:13, 14.

Blacksmith Herr Glaser at the forge. Reitinstitut von Neindorff. Each single hour in the saddle is supported by countless hours of groundwork involving a great variety of disciplines, each a highly specialized universe in itself. Photo, Dieter Schuchmann.

Recommended Reading

Riding Logic, Wilhelm Müseler. Published in German, *Reitlehre*, by Paul Parey Verlag. First published in English in 1937 by Methuen & Co. Ltd. London.

Horsemanship, Waldimar Seunig. Originally published in German in 1941, *Von der Koppel bis zur Kapriole,* by Wolfgang Krueger Verlag, reissued by Olms Verlag, Hildesheim, Germany. The English version first appeared in 1956, published by Doubleday & Company, Inc., New York; and by Robert Hale 1958; and by J. A. Allen & Co. Ltd. (in the *Allens Classic Series*) in 2003.

Dressage Riding, Richard L. Wätjen. 6th Edition, in German, published in 1966 by Paul Parey Verlag, Berlin and Hamburg. English edition published by J. A. Allen & Co. Ltd. London 1958.

The Way to Perfect Horsemanship, Üdo Bürger. First published in German as *Vollendete Reitkunst,* by Paul Parey Verlag, Berlin and Hamburg, in 1959. The English edition was published by J. A. Allen & Co. Ltd. London, in 1986, in the *Classics of Horsemanship* series; and in the *Allens Classic Series* 1998.

Reflections on Equestrian Art, Nuno Oliveira. Originally published in France in 1964 by Crépin-Leblonde et cie Editeurs, Paris. The English edition was published by J. A. Allen & Co. Ltd. in 1976.

Historically significant texts

Die Reitkunst im Bilde, Ludwig Koch. Originally published in 1928, Vienna. Reissued in 1976 by George Olms Verlag AG., Hildeshiem, Germany.

Gymnasium des Pferdes, Gustav Steinbrecht. Originally published in German in 1884. The eleventh German edition published by Dr. Rudolf Georgi, Aachen, Germany, in 1980. First published in English, *Gymnasium of the Horse*, in 1995 by Xenophon Press, Cleveland OH, United States. Translation by Helen K. Gibble.

Le Maneige Royal, Antoine de Pluvinel. First published in England, without English translation, in 1969 by J. A. Allen & Co. Ltd., London. The English translated version published by J. A. Allen & Co. Ltd., in 1989. The two J. A. Allen versions were based on an edition published in 1626 by Gottfried Müller in Braunschweig, Germany. English translation by Hilda Nelson.

École de Cavalerie, François Robichon de la Guérinière. Originally published in four parts in France, between 1729 and 1731, culminating in the best-known edition in 1733. Published in England in 1994 by J. A. Allen & Co. Ltd. London. Translated by Jack C. Schuman.

Horsemanship, Xenophon. Published in the German language in 1962, by Erich Hoffmann Verlag, Heidenheim, Germany. The English language edition translated by Professor Morris H. Morgan PhD, published and revised by J. A. Allen & Co. Ltd. in 1962.

Index of Illustrations

Line Drawings

Index

Use of this index: The first number before the period indicates the chapter. The number after the period indicates the section

B

D

F

G

H

I

N

O

Q

R

S

T

U

V

W

X

Y

Z

Abby ☆ Avanti ☆ Barkas ☆ Ben ☆ Bladey ☆ Bobbie ☆ Bolero
Buttons ☆ Carriba ☆ Charlie ☆ Chautelle ☆ Cricket
Dougal ☆ Patrick ☆ Pegasus ☆ Sparkie ☆ Tango
Tizzie ☆ Wellington

Aggie ☆ AJ (Javelin) ☆ Angel ☆ Bailey ☆ Bird ☆ Bonzo ☆ Bravo
Brigadier ☆ Bussell ☆ Caesar ☆ Cantanero ☆ Chevy ☆ Crisp
Evie ☆ Filo ☆ Fleur ☆ Foxy ☆ Fuzzie ☆ Gramschi ☆ GT ☆ Hoja
Ikaro ☆ Javelin ☆ Maverick ☆ Max ☆ Milo ☆ Moby ☆ Mopsy
Mouse ☆ Murphy ☆ Nig ☆ Nina ☆ Ollie ☆ Pay Day ☆ Pooh Bear
Profeta ☆ Rosie ☆ Russian ☆ Scrabble ☆ Shine ☆ Slipper
Spider ☆ Sunny Talisker ☆ Trinko ☆ William ☆ Yummie ☆ Zardi

Alee ☆ Almadera ☆ Ami ☆ Amy ☆ Angel ☆ Apollo ☆ Ari
Arrow ☆ Autumn ☆ Avy ☆ Bailey ☆ Beau ☆ Bijoux ☆ Brianna
Bronson ☆ Buki ☆ Casey ☆ Caz ☆ Champagne ☆ Chase ☆ Chaski
Chevallier ☆ Claro ☆ Coba ☆ Copper Penny ☆ CR ☆ Cyrano
Dakota ☆ Dejana ☆ Demetrius ☆ Denali ☆ Desiree ☆ Dom
Drosselmeyer ☆ Duckie ☆ Elite ☆ Fadra ☆ Fanny ☆ Finn ☆ Forest
Fox ☆ Fred ☆ Fritz ☆ Gaspari ☆ Giselle ☆ God Bless ☆ Hinde
Hope ☆ Instanz ☆ Juliette ☆ Koda ☆ Liberty ☆ Lilly ☆ Loken
Luke ☆ Magic ☆ Maya ☆ Milo ☆ Mr PS ☆ Olive ☆ O'Neil ☆ Otis
Paul Revere ☆ Peggy ☆ Peggy Sue ☆ Pono ☆ Porter ☆ Puca
Quincy ☆ Randy ☆ Rasheed ☆ Rose ☆ Rowan ☆ Sandy ☆ Sasha
Sawyer ☆ Shiloh ☆ Shimmer ☆ Simcha ☆ Spyder ☆ Star Fire
Stealth ☆ Stella ☆ Steward ☆ Tahoe ☆ Talamain ☆ Talula ☆ Tank
Tass ☆ Tatiana ☆ Tayasal ☆ Tess ☆ Tony ☆ Topsy ☆ Toto
Triftin ☆ Trilich ☆ Trixie ☆ Tuscany ☆ Virgil ☆ Winston
Zen ☆ Zepplin ☆ Zorro

Aldalair ☆ Armani ☆ Ben ☆ Bravo ☆ Breeze ☆ Bridge ☆ Ce Ce
Chantilly ☆ Crescendo ☆ Critic ☆ Darby ☆ Falstaff ☆ George
Gerisey ☆ Halla ☆ Hershy ☆ Indy ☆ IRA ☆ Irish ☆ Joe ☆ Kara
Katie ☆ Kora ☆ Lad ☆ Gunner ☆ Magic ☆ Mi Cameo ☆ Micky
Missy ☆ Morgan ☆ Mr Beau Char (Bowie) ☆ Mt View ☆ Notorio
Ochaco ☆ Pinyon ☆ Primavera ☆ Quinn ☆ Renee ☆ Rhody ☆ Rita
Rocky ☆ Royal Doulton ☆ Sailor ☆ Sam ☆ Shane ☆ Shiner ☆ Sig
Silver ☆ Skook ☆ Solitare ☆ Spot ☆ Streaker ☆ Tailor ☆ Tamara
The Bruce ☆ Toronado ☆ TW ☆ Tylar ☆ Windman

Ariette ☆ Balentino ☆ Bandit ☆ Begaern ☆ Bracken ☆ Cajun
Capitan ☆ Cappuccino ☆ Carla ☆ Cash ☆ Colera ☆ Dan ☆ Dancer
Ella ☆ Faehrte ☆ Ferrari ☆ Gandolf ☆ General ☆ Glen Nevis